The Perfect Sip

Foster Care to Freedom

By

Shay EL

Table of Contents

Dedication 1

Foreword 3

Chapter 1: Fresh Brew (Given Away) 5

Chapter 2: Scalding Water (Disconnected) 13

Chapter 3: The First Sip (Murder Trauma) 17

Chapter 4: Spills and Stains (Abuse and Neglect) 27

Chapter 5: Sugar (The Miracle) 39

Chapter 6: Expresso (Adopted) 45

Chapter 7: Caramel (A Youthful Champion) 59

Chapter 8: Half & Half (Identity Crisis) 65

Chapter 9: Sweet and Low (My Fathers Mistake) 77

Chapter 10: Stir Sticks (College Life) 87

Chapter 11: Caffeine (Relationship with God) 95

Chapter 12: Splenda (Reconnected) 117

Chapter 13: Coffee Filter (Facing Failure) 129

Chapter 14: Cravings (Making Better Choices) 139

Chapter 15: Sweet Life (Marriage) 153

Chapter 16: GoodAddiction (Flourish) 161

Benediction.. 171

Dedication

This book is dedicated to all the lost and forgotten children of the world, you *will* find your way.

Keep living. Trust God!

-Shay EL-

Foreword

There are many things in life I wouldn't have overcame if it wasn't for God and coffee. Both are just perfect and that's a fact. If you are a witness, please raise your favorite coffee container in the air and give God thanks by saying "thank you"! God loves being acknowledged first and He is worthy to be praised. His spirit is like an awakening aroma to the physical body and an energizer to the conscious mind. If you are unfamiliar to His flavor, allow me to be your spiritual barista, because everybody deserves to experience the taste of God's goodness. His word provides us with the ingredients that we need to take *The Perfect Sip* out of life. This book is my journey toward finding those ingredients This is my story written from my real-life experiences and is not to shame anybody because it wasn't for their involvement in my life there would be no me. As you read, may your soul be awakened, your spirit calmed, and your heart reassured that nothing was by chance and that everything truly is going to be alright. You control the taste of your coffee and the ability to change the flavor of your life. Make it good.

Chapter 1:

Fresh Brew

Woke up in an unfamiliar place. Staring into unfamiliar faces, I wondered if the people who I was looking at were my parents. Confused by the situation, I remember crying wanting my mom and dad. Tantrum after tantrum I was yerning for the love that every child deserves when brought into the world with innocense. No empathy, I was forced to come to terms with my reality rather quickly. This resulted in me acting out of anger on a daily basis and this is where the emotional trauma began.

Shay EL

My life as I knew it was in shambles. This was my oldest childhood memory. So who was I? The boy named Shay, the product of chaos and dysfunction. The king who was never given his crown. I was the boy who had a million questions but never understood what was going on. Yes, that is me! This was the moment I realized that I was different. But why? Out of the mouths of my early care givers, I was told that my mother sold and used cocaine. I was told that she sold her body in exchange for materials things and pleasure. I was told she had seven children with five different men. I was told that my father couldn't be found and was dead. Whether any of that was true or not, I had a whole family that was just gone, disappeared, extinct, ghost, vanished, Marco-polo, crickets, you get the point. I never knew them. Being born into a world that views your worth based on what you have and

don't have, I was predestined to be a "nobody" and my future pointed to failure. Initially what I thought was abandonment, I came to find out that I was taken away from my mother who was deemed as unstable to be adopted by another relative. Unfortunately, that did not happen, and I will explain why later. But here I was, a young boy who felt like the lowest person on the totem pole in society right next to the homeless. We are the offspring of the irresponsible. We are the forgotten. My perception at the time was tagged as being unwanted which made me feel like a reject and a misfit.

Understanding your value at an early age is a major benefit toward the confidence and attitude that we carry throughout life. Studies say that the first 7 years of a person's life are the most important in their development in life. I had low self-esteem for a long time which caused me to feel

invaluable. Being raised in the system can make you numb to a lot of things. The need for love, a warm bed, uninterrupted sleep, and a decent meal overrides your need for anything else. You'll be amazed at how young your survival instincts take over you and how quickly you adapt to dysfunction because that's all you have ever known. Looking back, I am so grateful that God placed himself and certain angels in my life to fill those voids. All I wanted was to be and feel genuinely loved as a child. The reassurance of my worthiness is what allowed me to love myself and feel comfortable writing this book. Only God can give us that.

At first, I felt embarrassed and afraid to share the things that I had been through. Being accustomed to procrastinating over the years, I felt like the biblical character of Jonah who was running away from his assignment. The negative mentality vanished once I saw and understood the bigger

picture. "Your story is not for you," those were God's words to me. However, I knew I had to gain peace with my past and peace with the predators in my life before sharing my story. Healing was required first. I also had to ask God for a clean heart, because it is hard to get a prayer through with an agitated spirit…more-less write a whole book. My purpose would not have been achieved with such imbalance in my inner being.

The theme of this book came about after taking a sip of the perfect cup of coffee I've ever made. Shockingly, I surprised myself. It was so on point that it made me pause and close my eyes for a moment. Now keep in mind, I worked third shift and often made coffee every night, but something about this particular coffee grind and blend of cream, sugar, and a pinch of cinnamon was just different. I was sipping so fast that I burned my lips a little bit and it didn't faze me. All I wanted was

another sip, and fortunately, it was the spark I needed to kick-start my story. That temporary pain didn't outweigh the delicious mastery of the brew I concocted that night. As I was drinking, I thought, "wow this is just like life, there is some initial pain or hardship then it is followed by beneficial satisfaction in the end that makes it all worth it". Isn't that the experience of childbirth? Isn't that the satisfaction of paying your dues and getting rewarded in the end? Isn't that the life cycle of a farmer who eventually enjoys the fruits of his labor? Isn't that the expectation for your discipline and dedication towards any investment, 401k policy, business venture or retirement? Good coffee will make you "deep" by the way, lol. I smiled and chose to relate the content of my life to everything related to coffee. I thank God for coffee, how about you?

Every sip is a milestone on the timeline of my life. Things started scalding hot but later cooled, becoming pleasant to the taste. Similar to a cup of freshly brewed coffee, I've been ground, mixed up, taken from my natural state, used for pleasure, discarded and replaced by something else and even devoured. When I got home, I told my wife that I had a clear direction for my book because as I stated earlier, "There are many things in life that I wouldn't have made it through without God and coffee." She threw her hands up and said, "You said a word right there hunny," and that was the final confirmation I needed to ascertain I was on the right path. God and coffee were the two constants in my adult life that gave me strength and comfort. They both delivered the perfect combination of spiritual energy and physical delight. God and coffee have gotten me through some of my worse days. Have you ever felt friendless, or worthless, or

used to the beyond belief? I dare you to pray and make yourself a good cup of coffee. Just try it and experience awesomeness.

Chapter 2:
Scalding Water

For a long time, I didn't know who I was nor what my purpose was. Did I even have the potential? Being taken away as a newborn mentally affected me in so many ways. I had a million questions that I never could get honest answers to, and they added to my brokenness. Where were my parents? When are they coming to get me? Why did they leave me? Why don't they love me? Do I look like them? I didn't realize this until I was much older, but I have spent most of my life in the middle of an identity crisis. Imagine

having to complete a puzzle without ever being shown the complete image. Now, imagine that all the puzzle pieces filled up a construction dump truck. That is how it feels not knowing who you truly are nor where you come from for the first 26 years (9,490 days) of your life.

Knowing who you are affects every other aspect of your life. It affects who you chose to love, how far you will go in life, how you allow people to treat you and most importantly, how you treat yourself as well. Take the Lion for example. He walks around fearless because he knows that he's the baddest beast in the jungle. The Lion doesn't sit around depressed because he doesn't have a fancy house and has to live outside. He's not hurt, because his mom left him to fend for himself in this cold world. He's not depressed because he's not skinny like a deer. Nope, he's a Lion, (the undisputed King of the Jungle), always ready to go up against anyone

The Perfect Sip

that puts him to the test. He is comfortable being everything God made him to be.

I often wondered why we as humans live life so confused and defeated while the animals naturally "get it." Fish swim, birds fly, frogs leap, cows moo, and humans (the so-called most intelligent) wander through life not knowing who they are or what they want to be. In most cases we have an idea of what we want to be but don't how to become what we desire to be. Unlike animals God has given us free will to do what we want to do and be whoever we want to be. You must ask God what he wants you to be. Life is all about the discovery and operating according to your purpose. You maybe wandering how to discover your purpose and that, my friend, is where true religion and spirituality begins. The answer is simple. Everything has to do with your connection and relationship to God. The animals never lost their connection, and as soon as humans

connect to God, our eyes will open, and we'll see ourselves for who we truly are. Looking back over my life, I see that God was with me through the scalding water periods. He was sustaining me through the beatings, hungry nights and failures that molded me into my purpose. The closer I drew to him, the more he showed me myself. What's even better is that God always saw the best in me even at my worst moments.

Chapter 3:
The First Sip

Unless you like your coffee with ice, everyone has to brace themselves for the first sip. My first sip came when I began to get true understandings of how things went down. I was born on August 3, 1988. This is the year God's blueprint manifested. I was informed that when I was born my mother had seven children and was a dope dealer on drugs from North Philly. Due to her dysfunctional environment and living arrangements at the time, I was also told that my siblings and I were split up between other family members and

associates. Amy was the person who took me home from the hospital after I was born. I was informed that Amy and my biological mother Patricia were related through Amy's husband. She had legal custody of me and my younger brother Alvin once he was born three years after me. I was also told he was born with drugs in his system.

My earliest memories of staying with Amy was at the age of five. I remember staying at 428 Turner St Allentown, PA with Alvin, Amy's oldest daughter Teresa, newborn daughter Rachel and an older foster child named Damon. I remember Teresa, Damon and I all attended Sacred Heart Elementary and were very close. Things were going on smoothly from what I can recall until Amy's boyfriend came into the picture. I can vividly remember him, and he was no good in my eyes. He often sexually abused and molested me. He always acted as if I was in trouble for something I did and

used that tactic to begin his malicious attacks on me. I was the type of child that never wanted to cause problems. I felt like if I did what I was told and stayed quiet that I would never have to worry about being sent anywhere. He always threatened to punish me or tell Amy about my alleged bad behavior. I was just a young child who liked to do what any normal five-year-old boy does. I was emotionally hurt by his actions. No matter what this monster accused me of I recall always screaming, "I'm sorry, I'm sorry". I had to pray those nightmares away. He sexually abused me because he knew I was helpless. Certain things are just too embarrassing to share. I cried and kept it a secret for years only to find out later that the same thing was happening to my little brother. I guess that's what happens when guardians are careless about the wolves they leave their children with. Amy was a loving but strict parent who did all that she could to

help raise the five children that were in her care. Imagine the stress. I never wanted to get in trouble or make her upset, therefore I was mostly controlled by fear. I never went and told her about these things because as a child I did not know better. No one had ever had "the talk" with me. No one had ever said that this was not right, and so in my mind, I felt like this was a part of trying to be a good boy and not cause trouble. Monsters take advantage of such vulnerability when looking for young prey to execute their evil deeds. I didn't know what was going on at the time, but this was the first monster somebody let in my life. I just wanted to play with my toys, watch my cartoons and stay out of trouble. This scarred me for life once I became older and learned about sex and the violation of private parts. At that point, my spirit was killed internally knowing that I had already been a victim amongst classmates who spoke with

The Perfect Sip

confidence about what they would do if someone ever tried that with them. I felt bad because I couldn't rewind time to apply the methods that were discussed. I never had a chance, and that ate me up for years as I buried all the emotional traumas I went through.

While at Amy's house, paranormal things would also happen that would creep me out. The older kids and I always saw moving shadows amongst the walls that did not come from any of us. We often heard our names being called, but when responding to see if anybody had called us, we found out that nobody said they did. There were several occasions where my sister, Teresa, screamed and asked us to get a broom to scare away the black cats that would always appear in her window sill. Mind you that we did not have any black cats. There was also a tree out front that was eventually cut down that I used to call the "Bat Tree" because it harbored bats.

There was just always an eerie feeling living in that house. I never liked going upstairs alone or for anything period. Although this sounds like a fiction horror story, this was real life for me. As a year passed, Amy's attitude began to change, and she was always unnecessarily angry. A new man was in her life who she often argued and fought with. She now also had a newborn, (Racheal), to take care of in addition to the other four children in the house and then there was an unknown factor that lurked the house. So, maybe that was why she was changing in her attitudes.

Looking back, I feel like the house had evil spirits in it that manifested in her and her boyfriend. There were times where Amy would get so angry with me for whatever reason to the point she would take me into the bathroom, put me in the tub on my back with my face directly under the water faucet and turn the water on while yelling madly at

me. This left me frightened, gagging, squirming and fighting to breathe. There was another incident at night when I may have been in trouble where she picked me up by my throat and slammed me on the hardwood floor. Instantly, I was knocked unconscious for a few minutes, and I woke up to her standing over me and then telling me to go back bed. I vividly remember this. This is not to say that she was a bad person because after all, she took me in, but I believe that whatever was going on in her life at the time negatively affected her behavior whether it was stress, exhaustion, frustration, evil spirits or the combination of them all. I am not one hundred percent sure what the cause was but all I can do is speak from my memory. Throughout the duration of the short period of time of me knowing her as a young a child I simply feared her. I truly believe the evil spirits that dwelled in the residence

were the cause of all of this. What happened next only confirmed my thoughts.

On the night of October 14, 1994, Amy was beaten and stabbed to death by her ex-boyfriend, Derick. Derick also stole Anita's car and $1,500 cash from her and fled from the house. I vividly remember everything till this day except for the actual altercation that occurred while I was asleep that night, thank God. I remember all these events as if it were yesterday. I recall waking up after wetting the bed afraid to tell Amy that it had occurred once again like the night before. As the other kids and I woke up and went downstairs to make breakfast, we all were stunned by the site of the horror in the living room. The first thing we saw was Amy's five-week-old baby, Rachel, strapped in her car seat still asleep on the couch. Blood spattered all over the walls, floors, and on the

chrome hose of the canister-type vacuum next to the sofa.

We immediately began calling for Amy frantically but received no response. I remember entering the kitchen, tiptoeing around the broken glass from the kitchen back door which led to the backyard and garage. As we began to realize what we thought transpired, we called the police immediately. The door to the cellar in the corner of the living room was open with the light still on and had blood footprints on the steps. None of us could bear the strength or bravery to go down the second set of steps to see if she was down there. The news article stated that the police found her body in the basement at around 7:30 am. According to the article that came out after the investigation, the police said that she was murdered between 11 pm on Oct 14 and 3 am the next morning. Derick's fingerprint and bloody sneaker footprint linked him

to the crime, and he was charged with criminal homicide, two counts of theft and receiving stolen property.

This tragedy stemmed from Amy and Derick's breakup due to his aggressive behavior and drug addiction. This was such a traumatic memory in our lives. God bless her soul. I always stay prayed up now and away from people that bring bad vibes and energy. I have seen firsthand the tragedy that comes with entertaining bad spirits therefore I constantly protect myself. As you can imagine, this was traumatizing for me as a child. I was thankful (even then), that he did not kill all of us that night. This was a very tragic day and according to public records and publications you can research the details of the true story by Googling: (The Murder of Anita Strickland-Womack). Acknowledging God's protection over us, I realized how blessed we were to have been spared from death that sorrowful

night. The result of her death put a significant distance between my biological family and me. This almost eliminated the possibility of reconnectionin the future. It was during that time in my life that my roots were firmly replanted, but the question pertained to whether it was for the better or worse? This was my first sip of life, and it burned.

Chapter 4:
Spills and Stains

After Amy's funeral, the five of us moved to Columbus, GA to live with Amy's sister, Jennifer and her husband Chris who had two children at the time. They took us in because Jennifer was Amy's sister and wanted to take care of her nieces. As far as me, Alvin and Damon we had nowhere else to go and they took us in as well. My biological family was nowhere to be found while all of this was happening. I was so happy with the fact that all of us got to stay together. While in Columbus, GA Jennifer and Chris moved us all into

a new six-bedroom house that sat on acres of land that had a half a mile-long driveway and a pool in the backyard. This was better than their former house which I remember them still moving things from. I remember the house vividly because when we arrived to retreive some items someone wrote the words Klu Klux Klan on the front steps. I recall asking what that ment which was my first lesson about racism. In addition to our new amazing home Chris and Jennifer bought new cars. Everything was new and improved but I began to wonder why me, and Alvin didn't receive anything new. Why did we still look raggedy? Why were we wearing hand-me-down clothes? Why did we never received any new school clothes or shoes like the other older kids? Why weren't we cared for? Nobody payed much attention to me. No quality time was spent with us and it began to be recognized when we attended school. It showed in our appearance, hygiene and

academics. Honestly, I felt like me and little brother Alvin were the runts of the litter and the male child version of Cinderella.

Our grades were below average, and the only help we got with our work was from my sister Teresa or Ms. Smith (Amy's Mother), when she came to visit. I ended up having to repeat the first grade. Both Jennifer and Ms. Smith were teachers so there should have been no reason for either of them to neglect our performance in school. Chris was cool. He was retired from the Army but had PTSD. I recall him being an Alabama Crimson Tide fan and playing football for a team in Georgia. He was very quiet and did not bond with me much but when we did it was awesome. I remember attending one of his football practices where he unfortunately tore his ACL. He was the first male figure in my life who I looked up to who introduced me to the game of football. We were a Dallas Cowboy fans. Chris

even got me hooked on getting waves in my hair and I was ecstatic when he bought me my first wave cap so that I could look just like him. I wish I got to know him better, but the love wasn't there.

We were unwanted and unkept point blank period. No excuses. Till this day, I remember in the second grade when I was specifically called out of the classroom by the principal and guidance counselor. They informed me about going on a special field trip with another black boy from another class. Unaware of where we were going, I told the principal and the guidance counselor that I did not receive a permission slip to bring home to be signed. For a minute, I thought I was about to be sent to an unknown place without my siblings, and I thought of every possible way to avoid making the trip. They told me that it was ok to come with them and that I would not get into any trouble. That special trip ended up being to the Valley Rescue

Mission to receive decent clothes that were clean and fitted, shoes that were our size that didn't have our toe popping out of them and new underwear as well. It felt good as a student in the second grade to have gone on a "Special Field Trip," receiving a big trash bag full of what I considered, "New Clothes" finally. It was when I became older that I realized what transpired that day and why I got punished when I came home with a big trash bag of clothes. Exposure. The mistreatment given to my younger brother and I were obvious to the point that the teachers and guidance counselors noticed our appearance and condition on a consistent bases while attending school. We stuck out like pepper in a tray of salt to the point they felt the needed to bring it to the principal's attention. Of course, they contacted our caregivers and began investigating our living conditions. I remember having to see the school counselor every week and having to lift my

shirt and pull my pants down periodically during private sessions for them to check for physical bruises which was perceived as an indication of abuse. This became frequent and uncomfortable. I told the school that I got in trouble for bringing home the bag of clothes. I was furious with the fact that I trusted the principal and guidance counselor to go on the trip to the trip and that I got punished for a situation that I was not responsible for.

After that school incident happened, it seemed that Jennifer and Chris resented having us (three boys) around even more and made plans for us to leave their household once that current school year ended. Our older sister, Teresa informed us about their plans and was very upset when she could not convince them to let us stay. Considering us as her younger brothers, Teresa was the only person who cared about us, looked out for us, stood up for us and even helped us with our school work. The

feelings were mutual, and she showed her strength in trying to help us the best way that she could. After all she was just a sixth-grade girl who lost her mother as well. Me and Alvin would wait for her to get off the bus after school and walking her home every day to protect her from the neighbor's loose dogs that would always bark at her aggressively as she walked up the half-mile long driveway. I remember running up the half mile long driveway as fast as I could to the house to get help when she fell off her bike riding down a steep hill along our driveway. She was my love, my big sister who always had my back. It was a very emotional moment as Jennifer went through with her plans as she intentionally sent us back up North to Pennsylvania to live with her mother, Ms. Smith who was in her upper 60's. Now there are many theories as to why me, Alvin and Damon were the only ones sent away. I know what the truth was.

Some would assume it was because all three of us boys were not directly related to the family. As a child I thought we were sent away because we were deemed as bad children and Jennifer and Chris didn't want anything to do with us. Some people have told me that they kept us around until the funds they recieved that were donated after Amy's passing ran out. Maybe, in a better light, they sent us away because they simply needed help. I find that hard to believe being that Jennifer ended up having 11 children after we were out of her life and my adopted mother showing me documents from the state that proved that she was getting paid monthly from the government in addition to the donation fund that was given to them. It could have possibly been the combination of theories. I'll simply leave it at that but like I said, me and Alvin know the truth. Fact remains that we were treated like crap. In the

mist of Jennifer and Chris's abundance we still looked like bums.

Upon our arrival in Pennsylvania, Ms. Smith was not the happiest to see us. She was a retired teacher who lived by herself for several decades, only having to take care of her elderly mother from time to time. Needless to say, after realizing that we were not going back down to Columbus, GA to stay with Jennifer. The alleged story was that we were supposed to stay with Ms.Smith for the summer but we ended staying for half a school year then we were put up for adoption. I can only assume that at her age, she physically and mentally did not have the desire to raise us. I recall Damon, the older foster care child, getting adopted first which left my brother and I to ourselves. Although upset and hurt from being separated from the older siblings, we pretty much had to fend for ourselves and stick together.

We eventually adjusted to his absence by meeting new kids and making new friends within the neighborhood. This was our first-time having neighbors we could interact with. At this time, I was seven or eight years old, and my brother was five. We attended Lower Marion Elementary School, which was where I met and made my first best friend, Jeffrey. We were in the same grade and next-door neighbors. Every day, all the kids in the neighborhood walked two blocks to school together, and for the first time, I experienced what being popular felt like. I was considered the coolest new kid on the block, known for being one of best street football and basketball player in the neighborhood. Kids would knock on our door after school to see if I could come out and play with them. Ms. Smith even found it humorous the way the girls would say my name when asking for me to come outside. Whether I could go outside or not

The Perfect Sip

depended on how much homework I had to do at the time. I can remember trying my best to get it done quickly, so I could get out that door to join my friends. I loved the attention because up until then, I had no idea that I was cute and to add to it, now I was cute and liked by all. People wanted me around, and that was just awesome! The girls would synchronize their greeting toward me and say "Heeeey...Shay" then laugh and wave. You couldn't tell me nothing!

The feeling of being important, loved or cared about was the best feeling in the world to me. I never felt it sincerely like I felt it from my peers at the time. It was almost at the point where I hated coming home every day because I loved the positive energy and kindness my friends showed me. I preferred being at school or outside in the neighborhood than being in Ms. Smith's home. Going home would feel like leaving the blissful

realm of paradise to slowly sink back into reality which consisted of a sense of worthlessness. This reality was magnified especially when I would get invited to Jeffrey's sleepover parties as I realized how good he and all his other friends had it. Although, his parents were divorced at the time, Jeffrey's father picked him up on the weekends and showed his unconditional love to him by spending time with him and buying him an abundance of toys. Through the eyes of a child who was not as fortunate as he was, I yearned to have Jeffrey's life even if his parents were not together. I was so amazed by all the toys he had. He literally had two rooms full of the newest toys and game systems. It was like Toys R Us at Jeffrey's house, and I could not help but feel jealous at all he had. I also felt ashamed, being that I was black, and he was white, and our lifestyles were different. My life wasn't neat like Jeffrey's. I felt like we spilled over onto

Jennifer's life and we were a stain on Ms. Smith's peace blanket that she was trying her best to get out. I spent a lot of time at Jeffrey's house. There, I got to see what love and being spoiled looked and felt like.

Chapter 5:

Sugar

It was in the middle of my third-grade year when my brother and I faced another transitional period. Ms. Smith was tired of putting up with us, and she made our stay uncomfortable. Maybe it was our behavior, our grades or simply just the everyday struggles and responsibility of taking care of two young boys at her age. I will never truly know, but it was obvious she was fed up. I recall Alvin getting into a lot of trouble at school on a consistent bases, and I also had my own share of bad conduct as well. In

retrospect, our behavior problems were probably due to everything we were going through and not having anybody to talk to. Our everyday life inside that home was very depressing. My brother was angry a lot and had trouble focusing in class. I recall getting into trouble for not doing my homework one time and for stealing lunch items from other classmate's lunch boxes. It may sound silly but going to school every day with a dry Bologna sandwich while the majority of the other kids enjoyed the items that were advertised on commercials made me feel poor and beneath them. Even the fact of bringing a brown paper bag to school while others had actual lunch boxes with whatever popular cartoon characters on it killed my spirit during lunch time. Indeed, I was engulfed by an inferiority complex.

Wishing for a better life, I spent countless nights lying on a soaked pillow from the tears that I shed,

The Perfect Sip

believing God's will toward my life was about to be revealed. Was I wrong for feeling this way? I did not know God at the time, but I knew how to cry out to Him through prayer. Back then, I considered talking to God as making a wish, and I knew how to make a wish. Therefore, when Ms. Smith threatened to get rid of us for the thousandth time, all I knew out of fear was to make wishes to God while staring at the stars. Fearful of going to an orphanage and heartbroken to the fact that I was going to be taken away from the friend's I loved, I began making wishes every night for a better life. I'm not exactly sure how long it was from the initial time Ms. Smith put my brother and I up for adoption to the time that we were informed about a couple that showed interest, but when it happened, I was so excited to the point I could not sleep. Thinking that my wishes came true, Ms. Smith was so cold-hearted that she killed all my happiness when she informed me that

the couple was only interested in my brother, Alvin at the time. Hearing that statement made my heart feel like it fell into my stomach. Although it was the truth, she also said it to be mean while literally getting enjoyment watching my spirit leave as soon as it lit up showing life again.

Immediately, I felt a combination of emotions to the point I felt sick, and I basically shut down. I cried to the point where I could no longer shed tears. My cries turned into long whimpers or deep, painful groans. In a state of sadness, I became, angry, and bitter to the point that I did not want to speak to anybody. Feeling a sense of panic and hopelessness, I thought in my head, "What about me God, don't leave me here." Not only did I not want to be separated from my brother, but I especially did not want to be alone in that house with her. I considered that being worse than a prison since we were already living there but

The Perfect Sip

without my brother, it would be a downgrade to a mental state of hell. During that time, I found myself running away to live with my friend Jeffrey which actually turned out good as his mom allowed me to stay the whole weekend. After that weekend ended, it was back to being a scared child that did not know where to turn or what to do. I remember spending much time with my brother each day as much as I could, trying to prepare myself for the moment we would get separated from each other. The possibility haunted me for weeks, however, the separation from my brother never happened. God revealed His glory and power to me when Regina and Sam decided to accept both of us. God showed me His love, mercy, and compassion by blessing my brother and me with good parents. This was the biggest blessing I'd ever received, and I was grateful every day that passed by. It was sweet like sugar. A new life with a new beginning. A breath of

fresh air. Oh, the joy that emanated from inside. It was in the year of 1998 that I first felt that God was real and had a breakthrough.

Chapter 6:

Expresso

My new life exploded with excitement and pure bliss. I recall being so happy and thankful thinking to myself how blessed and fortunate my brother and I were for still being together. I say this because the adoption process is similar to picking the ripest, best-looking fruit in a basket at the supermarket. It's not the easiest task, and it is time-consuming. Allow me to elaborate further. The adoption process begins with a couple having an interest in adopting a child. Each partner is screened by the adoption agency. They have to

pass drug and background checks, personal evaluation in addition to evaluating the residential environment and financial income. They diligently have to do this to ensure the safety and welfare of the child to make sure they are not just turning a child over into the hands of a child molester or sex offender. I'll say they honestly try not to put the child at risk, but I'm certain that wolves in sheep's clothing slide under the radar from time to time. Once the individuals involved passes the evaluations, they become acknowledged as qualified parents and are given large books of photos of children with a brief description of them consisting of age, gender, ethnicity, where they are from, eye color, hair color, etc. The potential guardians are given information pertaining to the child's parents, siblings, health records and environmental history so that they know exactly what they are getting themselves into as well.

The scariest aspect of being put up for adoption is the uncertainty of getting adopted into a loving family once you pass a certain age. The odds are slim, and statistics reveal that the younger the child, the better the chances he or she will be chosen by a family. Do you recall back in elementary school how two team captains would pick their teams based on who they felt would give them the best chances at winning? Well, that is how potential parents choose. They target a specific gender, age, ethnicity, and overall appearance of the child. Out of thousands of kids to choose from, what makes a child standout amongst them? Scary odds. Another good example consists of an athlete trying to go pro. How does an athlete stand out from thousands of other great candidates? I happened to be very fortunate because Regina and Sam initially only wanted to adopt my younger brother, Alvin. When they found out that I was his brother, they chose

not to split us apart since we were so close. I am so grateful for them. Imagining the alternative outcome is hurting and heartbreaking. It was already enough emotional trauma not knowing who my biological parents were. The thought of losing my brother after losing all my other siblings may have taken me out. But God. God had a plan, and Regina and Sam were a huge part in it.

Getting back to the introduction of my new life, it was like a double shot of expresso; it was absolutely amazing. I would describe my new mom as a gentle giant. She was 6'2, and although she didn't play much, I could instantly tell that she loved me. Never met a woman so kind and so loving. My new father was educated and articulate and even though he was a bit smaller in frame, they made the perfect couple. They were Ms. Piggy and Kermit the frog. My new life with my new parents began in the suburbs of Souderton PA. My brother

The Perfect Sip

and I were welcomed into another realm of life which we were never exposed to. The neighborhood was called Park Place, which consisted of nice three-story townhouses in a predominantly white neighborhood. Our house was very nice, clean, and stylish with a warm welcoming energy about it. I remember how excited I was to see my bedroom. We had a room that any kid would dream of. The walls were painted to our selection beforehand, and it was with our favorite color which was blue and green. We had new twin beds with a full bookshelf that came with it from Ikea furniture store, a whole sports theme from the bedspreads, rugs, pillows to the autographed framed pictures on the wall of Troy Aikman to Michael Jordan. I loved our aquarium fish tank and to top everything off was our stylish up to date wardrobe. I recall my mom throwing the bags that we arrived with in the trash even before we entered the house.

The best moment in the world I did experience was when my parents took us shoe shopping for the first time. Man let me tell you, coming from being custom to hand me downs and shoes from the Goodwill, I felt like I hit the lottery when I was given the opportunity to pick out any pair of shoes I wanted regardless of the price. It felt weird although I was happy. Amazed and shocked as if a slave owner randomly asked a field slave to have dinner with him out of pure love and kindness. I'm not saying I was a slave, but I'm trying to put in perspective of how I felt. I recall doing a double take saying "Are you sure I can pick out any pair I want?" I was just amazed and shocked, yet ever so thankful and humble. This was all over some shoes, but that moment was the best feeling in the world, in addition to everything that was given to my brother and I. I had the feeling kids get the night before Christmas simply taking in everything and

The Perfect Sip

how my life changed in the blink of an eye. That was just the tip of the iceberg.

Regina and Sam were the best. It was a little uncomfortable adjusting to calling them mom and dad, but after a while, I became at ease and comfortable with them. They both worked at Johnson & Johnson making good money to provide us with the best of everything. They both were active and members of bowling and tennis teams. My dad was a smart, nerdy, cool guy whom I admired so much due to his intelligence and the fact that he drag-raced. He was the only father figure in my life. I love him and very thankful for him being in my life. He and my uncle owned a racing team and had a garage shop in Philly. My dad had a cougar eliminator which ran an 11.50 down a quarter mile and my uncle Bernard had a 500 Ford Galaxy which ran in the upper nine-second range down the quarter-mile drag strip. Another great

childhood memory was going to the shop with him on weekends, watching them fix their cars and eating the best authentic Philly Cheese-steak sandwiches and hoagies for lunch. There was nothing in the world that could be compared to the weekends my dad took us racing — straight-up thrilling. The main race tracks we visited were Maple Grove or Atco Raceway. In my opinion, there was nothing better than the smell of racing fuel, burnt rubber, loud engines and checking out the variety of other race cars. Some race events would host Monster Trucks and Jet Cars as a special feature which I absolutely thought was cool as well. I am thankful for all the things my parents exposed me to as a child. It was as if they wanted to make up for all the unfortunate events and mistreatment that my brother and I went through before coming into their lives. I experienced real love and affection, and it did not spoil us either as they maintained

decorum in raising us. Oh no, I learned tough love as well when it came to discipline.

I must admit my brother and I were a little wild and needed a few lessons in following directions, respect, being on our best behavior and learning how not to take shortcuts in life by doing "half-ass work" as my father would say. I was in the third grade attending West Broad Street Elementary School in Souderton, PA when my new life picked up. The school was predominantly white with literally five black students, which really sucked because most of them were in lower grades. I admit I felt a bit uncomfortable and it was intimidating at first until I felt the love and acceptance from the students. It was funny but cool because it was as if I was a recruited athlete destined to bring their school a recess championship trophy or something. I was good at sports, and I didn't mind showing it. I wanted to play, all the time. That is what caused a

lot of disciplinary actions at home. It wasn't because of my behavior, but more so, I was always willing to put playtime and sports before my academics. The main house rule was strictly based on putting my grades first. My parents were very strict about that, and I'm very thankful for till this day. Both my parents would not only make sure that I did my homework but they also made sure I did it right. My skills were low, and therefore my mom and dad put all their efforts into teaching me good study habits, reading every day and testing me on what I read to make sure I was comprehending accurately. As soon as I got home from school, my butt was to sit down at the kitchen table to do my homework until it was complete and accurate. With two intelligent parents, it was a hard task getting adjusted to their standards, but they were very diligent about helping me. Oh, yea, there were many tears of frustration, and I did talk bad about them under my breath.

The Perfect Sip

There were plenty times I said that I hated them. I use to hate the failed attempts when kids in the neighborhood asked for me to play outside but I couldn't due to homework or book report assignments. Man, it was tuff for a kid like me, but it most definitely shaped and molded me for the better. Look at me now, you are reading my work.

My grades went up. My math, reading, and writing skills all went up. I went from being a C and D student to an honors student. The work was not easy, and I often liked to slack off at times, but my parents were always there to push me through and metaphorically beating a proper work ethic in my head every time my grades slipped. I give then all the credit for that. I remember those days like it was yesterday. I recall doing book reports on the books that were on my parent's summer break book list they made for me. I vividly remember Raisin in the Sun, which was cool and God-awful, Moby Dick,

which was boring and never caught my interest. While looking outside at all the kids enjoying summer, riding bikes, skateboarding, rollerblading, and enjoying all kinds of other fun stuff without the stress of school work, I could not go outside until I had completed a certain number of chapters. Book after book, I constantly had to work on book reports, perfecting the proper essay structure, grammar, pronunciation, spelling and once again comprehension of the material.

My parents already knew the storyline for each book all the way down to the characters, and this made it impossible to take shortcuts or present a false summary without having them instructing me to go back to re-read and make the necessary corrections to my mistakes. Their standards were solidly based on proficiency. I hated it, and although it sucked in the eyes of a third, fourth or fifth grader, it helped me a lot through school. Not

only did it help my academic achievements, but it also helped my confidence and outlook on school while in class. Still, once again, I felt happier at school because I felt free because my parents were very strict.

One of my parent's most effective punishments was stripping us from all privileges. No playing outside and watching TV and all we could do was to write a large number of long, redundant sentences on paper. Writing sentences all day was extremely tiring and it made me want to die. I would rather commit suicide, seriously. My dad told me that a butt whooping is only a temporary pain. Writing sentences was long, painful, tiresome, and embarrassing when company would come over. The worst punishment of sentences that I brought on myself was about 8,000 sentences which took me a whole summer too complete. The penalty was caused by the cutting a girl's picture out of another

classmate's yearbook simply because I liked her and did not have the money to pay for a yearbook. That was awful and was not even worth the picture of the girl. That was my most memorable punishment because it lasted so long. I recall even having dreams of writing sentences. From that summer on, I made sure I did not get into trouble that would put me in that predicament again. Even the feeling once I completed the sentences was a great relief. I felt like I served a year in jail or something. My attitude, as well as academics, did a one-eighty turn for the better after the first year with my new family.

Chapter 7:

Caramel

My fourth-grade year was very exciting for me. Many heartfelt events took place that year, and they were awesome. I never felt prouder than when my mom sat me down and asked me how I would feel about being a big brother to another sibling. I was like "Shoot yea" in my head, and I told her that I was excited and felt that it would be cool. The best part about the whole conversation was the fact that she told me that she was not going to have a baby but rather adopt another child. That meant that we didn't have to

wait nine months to experience this new joy. Yippppeeeee!! At that time, I didn't know why my mother couldn't have kids, but when I got older and realized the times that we lived in back then, I totally understood why she kept that part of her life to herself. About two weeks after the conversation, my little brother, Dre, who was three at the time, came into our family. He was the cutest, big-headed, curly-haired animated boy I ever knew. He was so full of life. He had a great imagination and was very creative. I didn't know much about his past life or his parents, but he was really cool in my book. Alvin and I spent lots of time with him, playing and helping him learn his name, numbers, colors, objects, etc. Often, he would do some silly things, and at random times, he had Alvin and me laughing. Another year later, my mom had the same conversation amongst the boys about accepting another member into the family, and that was when

The Perfect Sip

my youngest brother, Brian, came along. We got him when he was a baby, and I also didn't know much about his family's background, but I loved him like the others. He was a cute chubby baby who looked like a tub of caramel, and he liked to eat all the time and do what babies do.

I was proud of being the oldest of three boys but hated the fact that my parents came down harder on me because I was the oldest and had to shoulder some responsibilities. I had to lead by example and incorporate the famous Spiderman Movie line "With great power comes great responsibility" into my conscience. Well, not that much responsibility. I just had to set the example of what to do and what not to do, but it was all good. I still got to be a kid and do the things that I loved to do that brings me into another happy moment in my life.

Three words, Pop Warner Football. Football has always been my first love, so of course, I was eager to play when the opportunity came around. Earning the right to play due to my grades being acceptable, I was introduced to the real meaning of being dedicated to my passion and preparing for it. I began playing football for the Souderton Braves Pop Warner league. Before the school year began, my dad conditioned my brother and me during the summer before the upcoming season. He didn't believe in "half ass work," therefore he held us to our commitment in wanting to play football. That meant no quitting and putting in the work to perform well on and off the field.

Once again in a predominantly white suburban town, I was the only black kid on the team during the years I played there. I was taller and bigger than the majority of my teammates and had to be careful not to go over the weight limit in my division which

was 90lbs. My parents were dedicated and made the necessary sacrifices for me to be able to play, and they expected me to be dedicated to the game. Conditioning consisted of calisthenics, running and conditioning in the sun before the season. During that year, I had to earn my starting position (Offense/Defensive Tackle), over a girl who was a beast. As I improved, I gained a sense of confidence within myself while understanding what team work really meant. That year our team had five wins and five losses, making it to the Volunteer Bowl game in Tennessee. The following year, (1999), we went undefeated, winning a National Championship in Disney World. That was my first taste of sweet victory. Playing football taught me to be smart, tough, focused and to persevere. I must say, victory is sweet.

Chapter 8:

Half & Half

As a young African American male from North Philly, I was surprised by how easily I became accustomed to my Caucasian surroundings. Being the new kid on the block, all I wanted to do was to fit in and be accepted. The only way I knew I could make this happen was to be good at whatever my peers were interested in. I tried picking up on their lingo, dressing like them, listening to the same music and of course doing whatever they did. I had never paid any attention to hockey but the boys in my class and neighborhood

loved playing street hockey. So, I learned how to rollerblade first, then I learned how to control a puck while maneuvering a hockey stick in efforts to score. Once again, I never watched hockey, but because that was the main topic every day at the school lunch table, I began to watch the games just to be in the "know" category. I hated not knowing what everyone was talking about and how I barely related to the things that they were interested in. I recall every boy in my class had an Eric Lindros, Philadelphia Flyers jersey which made me want one too so that I could feel amongst *in* the crowd.

As I reached the fifth grade, I was pretty sure my parents took notice of all the new things that were changing me. While I was working hard to fit in with my peers, I was standing out just as hard with certain teachers as well. I stuck out like a hair on a biscuit. One of the biggest changes my parents saw was my attitude toward these two particular

teachers. I couldn't stand them and the way they treated me. One teacher made fun of my hair in front of the students by comparing it to a brillo pad. The other teacher instructed me as the only black kid in the chorus class to "sing better" since in his ignorant mind, I came from slavery during black history month. The teachers did this in front of the students, and it further made some of them feel comfortable in calling me names and teasing me. I was every black thing known to man. Having a dark chocolate skin didn't make it any better. I am not 100% sure, but I think that the issues I was having at school and the fact that I was trying too hard to fit in made my parents decide to move us to a more culturally balanced neighborhood. It's crazy how one or two bad apples can truly ruin the whole bunch. We moved to Atlanta, GA in 1999, toward the end of my fifth-grade year.

Moving to Atlanta was an emotional moment for me. Although school was getting a little awkward, I was still sad about leaving my neighborhood friends and teammates. To my surprise, one of my teachers threw a class pizza party on my behalf which made me feel like everything I could ever wish for. Each student signed a big banner, leaving personal, friendly comments along with their phone numbers. Some even gave me gifts and I was so shocked by their kind gestures. Maybe they did like me as a person, or maybe they just didn't want me around on a day to day basis. My closest friends and teammates also invited me over to their houses one last time just to have fun. Those experiences were so special because amongst them, I always mattered. I was considered popular and accepted by them. The fact that I was a member of the town's first Pop Warner National Championship football team made me the man in my neighborhood. The feeling

my teammates gave me was priceless, which made my movement to Atlanta prior to finishing the fifth-grade bittersweet.

We moved into a huge four-bedroom home in a newly developed neighborhood at the time on Rockbridge Rd called Park Place. Moving from a three-story townhouse in a neighborhood ironically called Park Place in Souderton, PA, I felt as if my parents bought a mansion. Having to jump right back into the swing of finishing fifth grade in a new school was a bit uncomfortable. Pine Ridge Elementary was the school I attended. Although the majority of the school was African American, I still stuck out like a sore thumb. It was definitely a culture shock. The kids were so rude and had no respect nor discipline for the teacher let alone others. Slang and sagging were the popular trends in the school. The girls had attitudes and were only into the bad boys who dressed like rappers. The

main thing I was teased about was how I spoke proper English and how I dressed like a so-called white boy to them. I could only assume that this meant not being hip to the hip-hop fashion trends while wearing my pants pulled up on my butt with a belt and my shirt tucked in. I was considered a lame and a square. I noticed how ignorant and mean the kids were. Another noticeable aspect of schools in the south was how far behind the education systems were compared to schools up north. They moved at a much slower pace on simple material that I learned within the first week of school up north. This was borderline depressing. I was teased there too and was not challenged enough. Once again, this resulted in me feeling like I needed to change who I was to adapt and fit in.

As I became more in tune with the culture, I fell in love with southern hip-hop music. My favorite artists at the time were Lil Wayne, the Hot Boyz,

The Perfect Sip

Mannie Fresh, the Big Timers, Lil Jon, the Eastside Boyz, Sisqo, and Snoop Dogg. Music was my stress reliever. A simple pen and notepad became my favorite tools in my personal life. Music combined with everyday emotions sparked a passion for writing poetry and my own music. I considered it as a way for me to vent. We didn't have cable television nor a game system throughout my elementary and middle school years. We couldn't watch any music video channels, and I felt a bit embarrassed any time a friend or a relative would visit because they would get bored easily. I couldn't relate to certain conversation topics because I was ignorant of what was going on in the world. Peers would look at me crazily whenever I told them about not seeing a certain movie that everyone had probably seen. As an adult, I still have not seen "Boyz In The Hood." I had no street cred and I was raised a square. It was like I wasn't black

enough to be considered black, yet discriminated on in the white suburbs for being black. So where do I fit in? This caused serious mental conflict as a child. I felt half and half. I had the right amount of preppy properness of a stereotypical white guy, but I didn't have enough cultural influence in me. I wasn't technically (hood) enough. I didn't have enough thug or flavor in me to be recognized and accepted amongst my peers of the same race. This really hurt my pride and ego and made me feel less of who I was. I wanted to be cool and popular like everybody else as a child. I hated feeling like an outcast.

Things began looking up though, during my eighth-grade year, the producers of the famous show, "60 Minutes," came to Atlanta to interview my family pertaining to our transition to the south. The focus was on the difference in lifestyles between living up North vs. living down South. My mother's friend who worked for the producers of

the show also suggested that our family should get engaged in their story segment. Mike Wallace and his crew set up their equipment in our living room but only interviewed my mom and me for some reasons. Mr. Wallace asked us different questions pertaining to being closer to our southern relatives, the school systems, employment, and southern culture. He was eager to hear about the lifestyle differences between the hemispheres. My favorite part of the experience was having the camera crew follow me back to football practice like a celebrity and getting to lay a guy out on film who used to bully me. It's funny how life works. Here, I was the lame of the new school, getting interviewed as if I was some big star. It was all eyes on deck, and I became popular that day.

As a child, no matter how well things were going, mentally, I always questioned who I was. I wondered why my biological mother gave my

brother and me up for adoption but kept the rest of her children to her care. I questioned why I was sexually molested, mistreated, neglected and abused as a kid. I questioned what my purpose was in life and why I didn't fit in with the crowd. I questioned why my adopted parents were so strict and hard on me, especially given their lifestyle. All of these questions pointed me in the direction toward building a relationship with God in an effort to heal and learn about myself.

As time passed, I began to receive answers to some of those questions. I became wise and more mature. My eyes were opened to what truly matters in life. It wasn't a priority in life to have the best clothes or shoes, being popular, knowing all the dance moves, memorizing every lyric to songs or knowing how to play the latest video games. Knowing how to do those things are fun and enjoyable in our spare time if you want to be an

The Perfect Sip

entertainer, but these skills are not required during a job interview. I recall a time when I was riding in the car with my parents rapping every lyric to a song, and as soon as it went off, my dad asked me a math question that I didn't know the answer to which shut me up. Although he killed my musical vibe at the moment, he taught me that knowing the lyrics to a song wasn't all that cool if I didn't know how to solve math problems. He also explained to me how I needed to put the same effort into memorizing my academic work in order to come out with the best grades. This gut check melted my vibe to sing another song while in the car with them. Who wants to get put on the spot with a left-field question while blissfully in our vibe? The lesson was to take my grades seriously if I wanted to succeed in the real world. We all know that the world is unfair and does not care whether you are

prepared or not. Life is going to just happen, and we must keep living.

Although, I hated the strictness of my parents, but as an adult, I thanked them for how they raised me. The success or failure of a person starts at home, and they did their best to give me a great foundation to build on. My parents raised me with high expectations and held me to high standards. Being the oldest of my siblings, I was always looked at as the example. I was mandated to do right and be right at all times in order to show the other kids how to be and live right. Imagine not knowing who you are and trying to show someone else who to be at the same time. It was indeed crazy, but I kept trying and never relented.

Chapter 9:

Sweet and Low

Life was going well in Atlanta, and things were sweet. As a family, we were finally adjusted to the area, added equity to our house through numerous projects. I was excelling in my academics, sports and even started getting invites to do things with friends I finally made. It was like the rug got pulled from underneath us out us so suddenly. My dad lost his job. He lost his good job over watching pornography while at work. The embarrassment and shame that it set on the family was really unbelievable. The thoughts that

developed from the reason he got fired were extremely disturbing in a sense. Pornography out of everything. He didn't get fired for discrimination, or not being qualified enough. He didn't get fired for not doing his job the right way, being late, failing a drug test, background check, stealing, sexual harassment, nor people not liking you but for looking at pornography on his computer while at work. All I could think about as my mom told me why he got fired with tears in her eyes was, was it that serious? This is something you would hear about in high school and laugh at the kid who got caught watching porn in class rather than a grown professional with a good job making good money. With total disregards to his family, this broke my mother's heart for the last time as it had happened before. I speak of this not to shame him but because it affected me, and I saw firsthand how hidden addictions can break a family. His unwise

The Perfect Sip

choice in decision making put us in a huge financial and emotional bind. I never saw my mom so hurt and disgusted. Everything they'd worked hard for was gone. We had to move out and sell our beautiful home. While figuring out the next move, my mom sold all of my father's most valuable things in order to keep up with the bills. My dad's brand-new F-250 Super Duty diesel truck got sold first followed by his '69 Cougar Eliminator (his drag racing car). She made him sell all his expensive guns, cd collections, tools, and the list went on. My mother went Goldie Hawn from "The First Wives Club" on him. As the oldest child, at the time, I lost respect for him because of his actions. I thought it was stupid and more so immature. I couldn't look at him the same way, especially after all the disciplinary punishments and petty over emphasized lectures he gave to me when it came to disciplining me prior to him getting fired. I kept

thinking about how he had brought hell into our lives all because he couldn't control himself. My mom told me how his employers repeatedly gave him warnings about him watching porn on the computer. Who does that? That was something most young male teens master when they go through puberty. Common sense even tells us where to look at it and where not to look at it. Even years after he messed up, my dad never really recovered as a man and a father to me. He became anti-social, stopped interacting with me and our relationship was never the same after that. I only can assume he felt ashamed, embarrassed and unworthy. Rather than recovering as a father, he turned into a sad dog in a sense, clinging to my mom's leg for dear life. I forgive him for his mistake because we all are human but I still needed my father.

The Perfect Sip

I loved and missed how my dad did stuff with us. He took us drag racing with him and his uncle at least once a month during the summer. My brother, Alvin and I loved reminiscing about going to their racing garage shop in Philly on the weekends to watch them fix on their cars. We loved how we use to walk around the corner from the shop to get the best Hoagies and Philly cheesesteaks for lunch. My father was the man who made me fall in love with the Philadelphia Eagles. I admired how he mastered any craftsmanship project around the house. When it came to intellect, he was a genius in my eyes. He wasn't as hip or up with the times as far as swag nor did he have any trace of thug in him. He was ten years older than my mom with a nerdy complex, but he was still cool in my eyes. Mom would always joke on him from time to time to make us laugh. Hilarious as it may seem, all those good days were gone as our lifestyle changed. Literally, my parents

were like Miss Piggy and Kermit the frog before the incident. My dad had a social life with his coworkers who played scheduled bowling and tennis games on Tuesdays and Thursdays. After his mistake, he changed drastically, and it was as if he forgot about me and my development as a man and as his oldest son. I still love and respect him for his involvement in my life, but he let me down as a leader, role model, and mentor.

My brothers and I had to move to different schools once again and on top of that, we dealt with the everyday tension between my parents. Hearing them fuss and fight brought my mind back to when I was living with Amy. I couldn't blame my mother, or I'd be hit too. I hated hearing loud yelling, cussing, things getting banged on, thrown and worst of all physical fights. It just was a domino effect emotionally on the family. We all had to suffer, but nobody suffered worse emotional hurt than my

mother Regina. She became the boss overnight and determined to lift our family back up on her own.

My parents never separated. Financially, they needed each other. My dad needed my mom to survive and my mom needed my dad's help with watching and taking care of us. My mom automatically became the leader and provider in the house. She told me that she would never have a man put her life in jeopardy again. Dad sank the ship, but my mother built another boat and kept sailing. This boat eventually became a yacht as my mother became the owner of her meeting event coordinator business. The connections my mother had amongst family, former coworkers and lifelong friends were beneficial toward assisting the family in our time of need. Those who loved us contributed in some form or fashion. In the midst of our transitioning, I saw my mother evolve into a stronger woman. Watching her business

progressively take off was very inspiring. I will always respect her for everything that she did for the family.

My mom showed me how to be a professional entrepreneur. I studied how she spoke when talking to clients. The pitch changes combined with her perfect balance of laughter exuberated a genuine yet professional verbal engagement. I observed her attitude, work ethic and demeanor as she conducted business. Never did I see my mother fold under pressure. She was not going to let the consequences of my father's mistakes keep us down anymore. Even the standards that she kept while we were struggling were still strongly intact. We never looked like what we were going through. We were always clean, and we never lived in a raggedy house regardless of the size. In 2003, we moved to Nashville Tennessee, and we lived in a nice double wide custom-built mobile home. I was grateful even

The Perfect Sip

when I got picked on by the kids on the first day of high school. When riding the bus to school, everybody could see where I lived. I never dressed like a bum, but my parents never bought me the popular clothes that my peers had. They did the best they could. I wore sneakers from a Rack Room shoe store, and I never wore a pair of Jordan's until I bought a pair in college. I was so ignorant toward the Jordan shoe game that I bought two fake pairs for 100 dollars and thought I was clean. I thought I found a plug that had the exclusive colors for a discounted price. Yea, I was that guy. Sheltered. I didn't have a cell phone, or computer until I was 18 and attending college. These days, children have the most relevant technology in their hands by the age of five. Whether you call it spoiled, privileged or necessary, I didn't have any of that until I was 18. My mother did a great job in keeping us afloat. I laugh about being lame, but I thank and applaud

her efforts. Even in our darkest moments she made things sweet when we were low.

Chapter 10:

Stir Sticks

My high school years were the years I had to define myself and discover my potentials. I attended Antioch High School near Nashville, TN. These were the years I had to start thinking about my future and what I wanted to do with my life. How did I want to live? What career path did I want to take? What college did I want to attend? What major? What financial aid can I get? Will my grades be good enough? Will my GPA and ACT scores be high enough? All of these questions fill the student's mind with

uncertainty. It was a bit scary. The pressure from the weight of life and reality began to rest on my shoulders, and I could feel the heaviness. Nobody has a clear pictured forecast of what their life is going to be like, but if you don't prepare for it, it will smack you like a freight train. This is why the pre-adulthood period is critical. We become of age and begin painting the future we envision. I would ponder over the correlation between what college had to offer over what I really wanted to do in life. I was always reassured that I had plenty of time to figure things out and that the most important thing was staying focused on making the best grades I could.

My dad always told me that if you fail to prepare then prepare to fail. Self-discovery takes time though, but in the end, it will be worth the wait. I encourage you never to doubt yourself nor become discouraged. Doubt is the usher to fear. I ended up

The Perfect Sip

taking the ACT Test three times, and my scores went from 17 to 18 then to 19. I was honestly ashamed to type this, but not only did I get accepted in college due to my 3.2 grade point average, but I was also able to rack up on scholarship money that paid for my college tuition all four years. Shame the devil, I graduated debt free.

I love how God used people to assist me in life when I finally had His favor. Tom Joyner was the radio personality that first shed light on the school I attended in Jackson, TN. Lane College opened in 1878 but was established in 1882. The school was named after co-founder, Methodist Bishop Isaac Lane who built the school to educate newly freed slaves with the preparation curriculum to become teachers and preachers. I attended from the years of 2007 to 2011. I love my alma mater because it gave me the chance to discover the power of my

potential. Lane had its good and bad attributes, but for the most part, I enjoyed my college years.

I had many great experiences but the first experience that I enjoyed as a college student, was feeling free. Like the 4th of July and Juneteenth holiday celebrations, I loved when I gained my independence. I felt extremely liberated. I didn't have to hear anybody's mouth or follow unnecessary rules. I was free to do whatever I wanted to do, and when I wanted to do it. Flunking was not an option at this level. My mom promised me a car after my freshmen year if my grades were good and the thought of going back home facing disappointment was a nightmare. There was no better feeling to me at that time than being foot lose and fancy-free.

College was an amazing awakening experience. You get to redefine yourself while experiencing

what it feels like to be an adult. We evolve throughout those four years or longer, eventually getting the hang of keeping up with the responsibilities of adulthood. I enjoyed those years and encouraged anyone to pursue a college degree if it is required for their preferred profession post-graduation. I say this because there are a lot of people who graduate college with a degree but have a job in a totally different categorized career field. My initial desired profession was physical therapy and sports medicine. Lane did not have any curriculum that was specifically directed toward sports medicine therefore, I chose the same major as my father which was biology. I figured at least it would give me more career options and advantages if I continue pursuing sports medicine.

I made it my business to stay busy and involved in activities on and off campus that was geared toward my desired profession at the time. I hated being bored and to avoid that, I chose to become a student athletic trainer. I wanted hands-on experience so that I could develop and obtain the necessary skills required to work effectively with athletes.

College is what you make of it. I took advantage of every opportunity available. During my experience of being a student athletic trainer, I was able to meet the Baltimore Ravens Super Bowl Champion kick returner, Jacoby Jones. Jacoby was drafted from Lane College by the Texans in 2007 for his special team skills. He was a cool guy and a clown for sure.

The best part about being a trainer was being able to travel out of state with the school's athletic

teams year-round. I was able to be excused from class on certain days depending on the away game schedules, I got to see different HBCU campuses and became popular amongst the players. Football season, however, was much harder than basketball season. I had more athletes to tend to, I had to deal with egos, attitudes, and diva-like personalities in addition to working in hot, cold and rainy weather conditions. Basketball season consisted of fewer athletes, games were always played indoors, and I was out of town every other day of the week to work on away games.

The objective is always to gain experience in the field you see yourself working in by any means. That was my initial goal. I knew that knowledge was power but sometimes, who you know can take you farther than what you know. Not only did I aim for the experience but for the reference connections as. I encourage every reader to find a way to stand out

amongst the competition. Start now and apply yourself.

I personally feel that we were not created to simply work, exist and die. We were made with a purpose inside all of us and to achieve more. We were born to thrive and be happy. College is where life began to stir for me. All I had been through and all I had been taught began to blend with what I wanted for myself.

Chapter 11:

Caffeine

I was proud of myself after my freshman year in college. I held my end of the deal that my mother made to me by maintaining A's and B's. Receiving my first car as a reward felt like I had earned my wings. Having my own car granted me access to another level of freedom. It was a milestone in my life as it is in everyone's life. Do you remember the feeling you had when you received your first car? This was huge for me and an overwhelming experience. Having my own transportation meant I more had to depend on

anybody for a ride, no more waiting and having to catch a bus, no more paying folks to take me places when I needed to get things done and the biggest benefit was being able to get up and go places anytime I wanted to. My mom bought me a used all white Chevy Corsica that I personally named "CC." Why do we give our cars personal names? I actually don't know. I guess for attachment purposes. I did not care if I had a used or new car. As long as it wasn't a junk-box, and it got me from point A to point B, had air, heat and a CD player I was happy and content. A car is like gold to a college student. I was thankful and more importantly appreciative that my mom bought me my first car rather than me having to buy it myself. However, this is where responsibility along with the reality of adulthood crashed the party of blissful euphoria. My car became my first major responsibility besides school.

Relating to the Bible, the first thing that God gave man was responsibility. Before Adam was given a wife, God instructed him to manage the animals and the upkeep of the garden. It was only after God saw the worthiness and responsible behavior of Adam that He gave him a wife, so he would not be lonely. Most people don't understand how God won't bless them with certain things that we desire if He does not see that we are ready to handle them. Having my first car was my first responsibility and introduction to adulthood. My life took a bit of a detour after my sophomore year. This was the moment in time where I wanted to be grown and move off campus. I was tired of having to abide by the campus dorm rules. As residents, we had a midnight curfew, visitation from the opposite sex was not allowed, random room inspections were always in effect, we had open dorm showers which was uncomfortable and having to tolerate

loud music and immature behavior from others became totally annoying. It felt like jail in a sense. I was fed up, plus staying off campus knocked four thousand dollars off my tuition per semester. Can you say money in my pockets? Having an apartment off campus was my goal. I had a car and a job. All I needed was a responsible roommate that I could trust to go half on an apartment with me. Unfortunately, this was when real life, that adult life, and that "free" life hit me like a ton of bricks.

I took every aspect of my life seriously, and I didn't play about my rent money. Never in my life did I ever imagine getting put in jail five times. Yes, you read that correctly. It was that bad. Naturally, I am a nice guy, but like most nice guys, people took my kindness for weakness. The first time I went to jail was in an ugly situation where I walked in on my girlfriend cheating on me with another guy. I absolutely lost my mind, and in the heat of the

The Perfect Sip

moment, I slapped fire from her a few times and pulled out my gun. While she was crying, snorting and apologizing, I realized that this fool was still there. This clown sat comfortably on the couch in the other room as if he was waiting on us to finish arguing. Only the Lord knows what he was thinking. I guess he was feeling himself, but that ego left his body quick, fast and in a hurry as soon as I pointed my gun at him. Never have I seen a person go from acting so hard to running for their dear life. I did not have any intention of shooting him, but the audacity of his actions threw fuel on the fire. It was comical as I watched how he ran out of the house fumbling with his keys trying to unlock his car while looking back at me as I chased him outside. Any other man in their right mind would have left not wanting to be a part of that kind of drama, but it was not just so for him. He needed the pistol escort package out. I ended up in jail that day.

The betrayal & disrespect caused my heart to turn cold. For the first time, I understood how good men get their hearts broken and eventually turn into players and promiscuous people. Sometimes, it is due to their experiences of being hurt to the core.

The second and third time I went to jail was due to fighting trifling roommates on two different occasions, who would steal from me and secretly not uphold their end on the bills. This caused utilities to get cut off, and eviction notices to be placed on our doors. Their irresponsible behavior put my survival and livelihood at risk. I was not trying to be homeless and helpless. They did not have the same mentality that I had when it came toward being independent and responsible enough to stay off campus. I had to introduce them to these hands. The lesson out of that experience was learning how to use discernment when picking good roommates. The after effect once again was having

The Perfect Sip

to come out of pocket toward to pay the court fines, bailing myself out of jail and being on probation. To add insult to injury, nobody had time for that nor the money to waste. This led to the stupidity of my fourth charge which was shoplifting. I had to buy new work shoes and deodorant during a period between paychecks where I was low on money. Unfortunately, I only had enough to purchase the shoes, and so I made a choice to steal the deodorant. Stupid right? I know. However, I had to have my favorite Old Spice deodorant and more importantly I did not want to be walking around musty. Thought I was slick by putting them inside the shoes, they saw me on camera, and I momentarily tricked the security when they stopped me by showing the receipt and the opened box of shoes. They had to look back at the tape and searched the bathroom, and they saw me going in hoping that I purposely left it hidden so that I could

come back for it. I simply put it inside the shoe along with the packing paper. It took them twenty minutes to realize that I hid them in the shoe. I got caught and spent a night in jail and bonded myself out the next day. Fortunately, I had a friend who was a bail bondsman and my barber that always signed for me and backed me up. This was always a blessing saving me from a thousand questions being asked by my parents. It didn't save me from embarrassment though. Shaking my head.

You would have thought I learned from my past experiences. I shocked myself at how many times I went to jail. Although, the charges I've gotten were all misdemeanors, I started asking God if being in foster care for the first 8-9 years of my life made me develop into a criminal. I often wondered if the circumstances that I was born into doomed me for life. Was I a criminal or just a normal human being who was tired of getting mistreated? Was I a

criminal or was I a normal human being who reacted how most would react out of anger? Did I have unresolved anger issues? Did I need more therapy or counseling? Was I a bad person more importantly? I was raised to be better than that after getting adopted, yet I was never shown how to diffuse my anger and frustrations. Writing in a journal was not enough. Keep in mind how strict my parents were and how sheltered I was. As kids, we would get hit with whatever mom laid her hands on whenever she was mad, and it came to discipline. I remember having to call the police on Regina for hitting me with a skillet after she found a love letter I wrote to a white girl back in high school. She hit me so hard that she broke the skillet. I recall times where I got smacked in the back of my neck while doing the dishes for not doing them properly and for having the water being cold. Mind you Regina was 6'2 and 250 plus pounds and she was bigger

than my dad, bigger than all of us. That smack got filed into my memory very well. Family members addressed her as the Big Aunt ReRe being that there were two Regina's in the family. I never properly learned how to handle certain situations properly. My thought process was to teach whoever did me wrong not to ever do it again. Subconsciously that behavior was imbibed in me. If you do wrong by me, embarrass me or go against the established rules, the consequences would be discipline. Although, I was given a better opportunity to make something of myself in life, I was never taught how to properly handle negative people whose intentions were so destructive. Avoid them, yes, but we never know their hidden intentions until something bad happens. By then, it was too late and the damage was already done. I used to get so mad and embarrassed when kids would tell me that Regina was a man or transgender due to their perception.

The Perfect Sip

Rumors would get spread and once again I would get picked on which instinctively would trigger rage from within. I was not about to allow them to disrespect the woman who gave four boys a better chance at life. Rather than acting on it I would internalize it and be mad. See you must be careful with "mad" because "mad" will take you places and then leave you there. Mad will have you in jail ruining your chances at a decent life, then after a few hours, you will discover that you are not even mad anymore, but you're still in trouble. The wild Childhood Shay, who had to fend for himself resurfaced a lot during my early transitioning years into adulthood. All I knew was how to stand up for myself, defend myself, and how to secretly get payback toward people who caused me any harm.

Violent and abusive behavior pertaining to discipline was all that I was shown by my former caretakers in foster care and by my adoptive

parents. I know it may come off as an excuse, but it's not. That's just the simple truth. Now that I am wiser, I see how fear affects everybody both good and bad. Fear is used for control and serves as an intimidating mental threat. My fear at the time was being a homeless college student that flunked and failed. I also wanted to be happy with whoever I was with. Unfortunately, my choices in those people led to a lot of my minor setbacks of which my detentions were of such. My reaction to their actions made it worse as I mimicked the behaviors of those who disciplined me.

I found out quickly that living independently was quite challenging when making minimum wage and going to school. Despite everything that I was dealing with in school, I did not want to have to go back home. I wanted to make it on my own and have my own with all the credits to my effectiveness. Unfortunately, things only got worse,

The Perfect Sip

and I found myself in jail for the fifth and last time (as I promised myself). It was a girlfriend issue again. I found out that I was being cheated on again and I slapped her and threw her phone at her face. I don't glorify abuse nor domestic violence, but I just snapped after reading those raunchy sexual text messages this man sent at 2 am in the morning. For anybody reading this, I will advise you to please leave a relationship before it gets violent. When you see certain traits in people, just run for the hills and never look back. I was ashamed of my actions. I would never hit a woman now, but back then, I was just tired of getting played seemingly by everybody. Have you ever caught a partner cheating? Have you presented the evidence to them, and you listen to how they fumble to put together a lie? They stall for time and get the "stuck on stupid" look while trying to figure their way out after getting caught. Don't you hate how they try to play you like you are stupid

even going to the extreme by having a friend or family member lie for them? It will certainly drive you crazy. To add insult to injury, I had to take a 6-month domestic violence class in addition to facing the all too familiar court process. Once again, I had to spend money to bail myself out of jail and being put on probation. That kind of pain burns through to your soul causing trust issues and insecurities that may last a lifetime.

No matter how good my grades were in school at the time, all these arrests put stains on my record and destroyed my reputation. I knew then that even though I was set to graduate with honors, my criminal record was going to be a major problem for me. It was not good to fall into these types of destructive patterns as they will place your reputation on high risk. At one point in time, I felt like I was cursed at how almost every year while in college, I kept finding myself in a jail cell overnight,

inside a courtroom, outside doing community service and in front of a probation officer. Fed up with how I kept getting sucked back in the cycle of trouble, I had my second serious life conversation with God. This time, it was different from a prayer as I vented all my frustrations and concerns to Him for hours. I started by admitting my wrongs and asking God for forgiveness, guidance and more importantly for wisdom. The roadblock many of us get stuck and struggle with is the 'how' part. I wanted and needed God's intervention as fast I could. My life was full of stress, anxiety, and pressure. I almost got kicked out of school due to my off-campus problems, and I was beginning to be really depressed. I regretted not experiencing the college life at a university. The small town of Jackson, TN alone is a depressing town for a young adult who wished to thrive and grow. The town only comforted the natives who have lived there

their whole lives. The school was in the "Hood" right around the corner from the Lincoln Court projects where crime was frequent. Surrounded by poverty all those four years, I began to settle in that type of mindset of, "Why didn't you transfer, Shay?" My answer was simple, I did not want to prolong my time being in college. I did not want to have to retake certain classes to regain credits nor mess up my tuition situation. I had to keep telling myself to tuff it out. All my high hopes, desires and dreams diminished, and reality was rapidly closing in on me. Nothing really motivated me or made me happy anymore besides weed, sex, and money. So, I asked God for help to get out of my predicaments. I wanted joy back in my life and only knew that God could give it to me.

Why are you reviling all your dirt, Shay? Because my life has not been squeaky clean, and I did not want my testimony to become sugar coated like

most people do. Folks would only tell you a G-Rated version of their testimony. I'm giving you the real story to my life's sojourn. There were periods in my life where I simply was dead wrong. I am the type of person who likes to be transparent, and I own the fact that I am deeply flawed. I am at peace with everything that I talk about in this book because it made me who I am today. Truth and transparency is where true inspiration originates. We initially admire something, then we appreciate it even more when we see the details of how it was made. Think of the people who inspire you and why they inspire you. You will see the brilliance in who they are and what they have become given certain circumstances. Their story inspires you, and I pray that mine will be amongst your favorites as well. Writing this book has given me closure, and I want it to help others as I let my voice out. My testimony is to honor God's will for my life and to

elaborate on how He has helped me from within. Therefore, I decided to be as authentic as possible. It is true to say that God is always willing to help anybody who calls on His name with a sincere desire to build a relationship with Him.

What I initially perceived as dirt in my life turned out to be my coffee grains. Similar to coffee, we have to go through a grinding process in order to extract the beneficial goodness that we all possess, and God serves as the caffeine within those grains. He is the caffeine that jumpstarts our mind, body and soul. I definitely feel more awake having Him in my life. I speak to God always like I speak to a friend. Sometimes, I hash it out with Him but for the most part I find myself always thanking Him regardless of my current circumstances. Tired from living under storm clouds, I knew I needed to strengthen my relationship with God. I was tired of doing things my way, stumbling and running into

The Perfect Sip

dead ends. I was tired of getting in trouble and was tired of having the wrong people in my life. In order to see sunshine once again, I informed my Heavenly Father that I needed His help. Having free will and doing things my way was not cutting it. I wanted to regain peace, joy and prosperity in my life. Those gifts are priceless, and I knew that only God could deliver them. He was the only source that truly understood what I was going through.

When I came to Him in truth, He responded to me. He heard me loud and clear. I wanted my zeal to be reignited with His abundant love. I needed a spiritual and physical boost of energy. I knew I had to become submissive to God and His will for my life. I believe God feels our hurt and frustration when we vent in prayer. He feels our energy similar to how we rush to the aid of any of our loved ones when they are hurt or in need. With me wanting a real breakthrough, God had to take me away from

the church. My spirituality mixed with messages based on personal agendas within the church left me confused and spiritually starving. We all know who the author of confusion is, right? God wanted me to get to know him more intimately. This meant longer intimate prayers, more frequent conversations, and fasting. As I reconnected with God, the familiar feeling of his unconditional love resurfaced once again and overwhelmed me. It was as if it never left. The more I was distracted by the world, the farther I was from God. Over the years, I learned that having a real relationship with God consist of being spiritually conscious. Unfortunately, I was only conscious of the mistakes I made in my life. I always felt like I was a mistake brought into the world, however, God saw the best in me and only the best. He transformed my pessimistic mentality into one of royalty. God told me not to think or look at myself as a mistake but

as a special unique vessel. God didn't care about any of my past mistakes. His plans were bigger than that, and it was evident in His continuous love toward me. God showed me that He is more concerned about our state of living, therefore, I asked Him to remove everything that was hindering my progress. In my case he wanted me to continue moving in the direction of my assignment and to remain focused. God is, was and will always be the caffeine that my spirit needs daily to stay woke and function according to His will.

Chapter 12:

Splenda

After reconnecting with God, my life got a bit sweeter. When you hear people say God is an on-time God, believe them. Sweet! He may not come when you want Him to, but He is truly always on time. I definitely needed God throughout my last two years in college. He assisted me first by restoring internal peace in my heart. I was able to refocus on graduating while getting blessed with the approval for my own apartment after leaving my former no good roommates. Second, God blessed me by preventing

an expulsion due to my off-campus run-ins with the law. Third, He allowed more positive people to surround me which did inspire me and changed my negative mindset. Upperclassmen fraternity recruiters saw me as a good potential prospect and selected me to join a line of ten other aspirants for the pledging process. Pledging a fraternity or sorority is pretty much like the college version of army boot camp or joining a gang. You undergo an initiation process that disciplines you by testing your physical and mental strength. I completed the process respectfully earning my status as a member of the distinguished and most prestigious brothers of Alpha Phi Alpha fraternity incorporated. My choice in this particular fraternity was based on the relationships I had with members who pledged before me. I liked how they carried themselves and after researching how Alpha Phi Alpha fraternity's aim stood for manly deeds, scholarship and love for

all mankind, I knew that it was right for me. The experience of making it through a long difficult process with strangers was entirely life-changing. I learned what brotherhood meant in addition to understanding what it means to be a successful, respectable African American man in society.

Graduating from college was a major accomplishment for me. In my eyes, I viewed earning my degree as taking down Goliath with my slingshot. The journey was tough, and after four long years, I was burned out of school. The best graduation gift was being able to get a nice apartment for my first-born son two weeks after I walked across the stage receiving my degree in biology. He was a preemie. He came a month and a half early. He weighed three pounds two ounces. The gift of a son was special to me because it gave me the opportunity to be the type of father that I always wanted to be, yet never had. The appearance

of my son warmed my heart because he looked so much like me. I never knew what I looked like as a baby nor a toddler because until later in life, the comparison was special. Seeing him grow up has been everything to me. His facial hair as a preemie made me nervous at first because I didn't expect it. He came so early delivered through an emergency C-section, and he still needed to develop. I had a strong appreciation for doctors, nurses and modern technology. Watching how the nurses in the N.I.C.U (Neonatal Intensive Care Unit) took care of my tiny little human was Godly. Being able to help feed and change diapers on such a small body was a little scary though, but it was welcoming. I was nervous as a first-time father. I was even more nervous watching how the nurses effortlessly yet borderline violently tended to the preemies. Everything was perfectly fine, but it was the rate that they did things while being totally numb to all

the crying. Everything looked like it hurt to the touch. They maneuvered around all those sensors, wires and monitors like they weren't even there. Watching them gave me the confidence that I needed to do my part as a dad. Welcome to fatherhood. It felt good having a new purpose and new energy in my life.

I never knew what God had in store for me at the time, but he opened the flood gates of blessings. I went from being left in the hospital after I was born, to being right there to welcome my son into this world. The generational curse of abandonment was broken. God is good, and I thank Him for that. I had my son, an ok job as a physical therapy tech out of college, no student debt and above all, God proved to me that He was real by answering the prayer I prayed when I was young. I simply wanted to know who my biological family was. I was 25 years old at the time when God felt I was ready for

the answer to get revealed. I almost missed my blessing at the hands of my son's mother who found the letter in a few week-old piles of mail that she had in her car. She could have easily looked over it and threw it away. Instead God prevented that from happening. The letter came from my older brother, Shakur, who had written me introducing himself and explaining everything that happened when I was younger and how he never stopped looking for me. He told me about my two older brothers (Dre and Marvin), my older sister (Sherry) and youngest brother (Shakari). I instantly began shedding tears of joy for a variety of reasons. It took 25 years for me to see where and who I come from. Discovering that I had closely aged siblings was also exciting. God finally answered that special prayer request I made when I was twelve years old. I met my biological family members through Facebook and had plenty of phone

The Perfect Sip

conversations catching up with them. There was a lot of relatives who were excited to hear from me. They were all full of curiosity as if I was a new animal exhibit at their local zoo. It felt good, yet awkward at the same time. Personally, I felt like a misfit that turned into royalty like Moses when his mother put him in a basket in the river to escape death. Moses was adopted by the pharaoh's family after he was found on the river bank and became the prince of Egypt. Prior to my brother's successful attempt of finding me, I was under the impression that both my biological parents were dead. It was exciting speaking to everybody although we were all strangers as we hadn't met. There was a lot of apologizing on my biological mother's behalf. She admitted to every wrong decision she made in my life expressing her intentions, yet was happy to see how I turned out. She explained how she sold drugs in North

Philadelphia in the late '80s and how she messed up her life when she became a drug user. She also explained how she fought to get clean to redeem herself by the court system but expressed how it was too late to make a fast turnaround. My biological mom explained how she tried to keep in touch with us by contacting Regina, but she wouldn't allow us to communicate. Both sides held tight to their own versions of what did and didn't happen, but I was not worried about any of that because the damage had already been done. I was no longer worried about whose fault it was, all I just wanted was to reconnect and start afresh with my bloodline. I was curious about where my dad was, especially since I knew he was alive. It was about a year later that she ran into my biological dad at a family member's funeral and got his number for me. The messed-up thing about it was that it took 26 years for me to speak to my dad who didn't

know I existed until that moment. My mother didn't tell him that I was his child, therefore, I could not blame him for being absent. Crazy and awkward right? Two grown strangers, father, and son. One can only assume the lifestyle of a female drug dealer who had an addiction with multiple kids. Chaotic and dysfunctional. Who am I to judge though, I was just the consequence of irresponsible actions from irresponsible adults. This was the reason God intervened. My life could have turned out differently had I been raised in that environment and for that I am grateful.

My biological father's last name is Savage. If I had his last name, it would definitely portray my character when I'm angry. When we spoke, it was emotional like every other conversation I had with other relatives I spoke with at that time. He expressed how I sounded like him when he was 26 years old and that I looked like him. He seemed

excited to have a son and a grandson, yet he was still skeptical if I was truly his child. He mentioned that he wanted a blood test done for verification. We never made it that far. I kept in touch for a few months before his number changed and I never heard from him again. He would always tell me not to take any unnecessary crap from anybody. He seemed very stuck in his ways as if he had a chip on his shoulder. He told me he was on probation at the time for threatening to kill a lady he was involved with. He also mentioned that he had a roommate who he kicked out of his house and told me that he would come see me when he got off probation at the time. In my head, I thought it was crazy how he was going through the same court trouble I had gotten out of at the time but at a way much older age. It was the son who had to advise the dad. He informed me that he lived in Reading Pennsylvania, although he never gave me an exact address. It was

bittersweet losing touch with him, but at least I got to speak to him. I believe God strategically places people in your life for reasons and seasons. My relationship over the years with the rest of my siblings has been kept at a distance through social media. Nobody made any attempt to meet me in person, and so I felt that was the best way to keep it. I understand how we all have our own lives and have financial responsibilities, but I did feel that at least my mother owed me a visit. I feel that if I had a long lost relative or child, I would make it my priority to meet them in person or at least communicate with them every now and then to show some love. I don't hold any resentment in my heart because God placed it in my spirit to go see them in person. At the moment, I'm good and at peace with where I'm at. I thank God for allowing me to connect with them because it filled a void in my history timeline. It was a blessing. Many foster

care and adopted children never reconnect with their families. I was one of the lucky ones. I was unfamiliar with who I was and where I came from but over time, I had to understand that my identity pertains to how God sees me and not so much as to the people and environment I came from. I never thought that I would ever know who my parents and other siblings were, but God had it all in His plans.

Chapter 13:
Coffee Filter

Four years after graduating, my life started its spin cycle. The struggle of getting to where I wanted to be in life was difficult. Therefore, you should properly prepare and be financially stable before having kids. I take the blame for where I was in life though. I began to settle for a bad relationship, a dead-end job (just to say I had one) and borderline poverty. Nothing about Jackson, TN inspired me or sparked any interest in toward what my vision was. Everybody that I went to college with all moved out of Jackson not long

after we graduated. I felt left behind, stuck, off course, and lost. I felt bad as a father and a provider. My children's mother and I were constantly getting into it with each other and I began feeling bullied and belittled as a man. Frustration from both ends kept the tension in our relationship and it impacted negatively on us. We were engaged at one point and she wanted to get married but my spirit didn't feel it was right nor the right timing. I began telling myself to get married anyway, and things will magically get better in an instant. My spirit was not at peace. People make mistakes in life when their reasons for getting married are anything besides pure love. Your choice to get married should never come forth from pressure. I was not ready personally nor did I like the way she treated me. At this point, we both had cheated on each other and had developed severe trust issues and insecurities. "Why marry someone

you don't trust?" I kept telling myself. Plus, we were raised differently and came from two different backgrounds. She was from Jackson, TN and grew up in the Lincoln Court projects whereas I grew up in the suburbs. I'm not saying that one is better than the other, because both places come with their own set of issues, but I am saying that we had two different set of standards and mindsets and it was always going to be a challenge inculcating them together. The comparison between the mother that raised me and the mother that raised her was completely different. As I gained more understanding of life by going to church, I learned that two people must be equally yoked before and after marriage and must be on the same page. In our relationship, we simply clashed and bashed and that was not healthy for the kids nor for us as we had two boys now.

We separated on Father's Day in 2015 and I moved in with my parents who lived two hours away in Columbia, TN. I was sad about leaving my kids and not waking up to them for the first few months after getting readjusted to my new life. I thanked God throughout this time because I knew I needed help to make changes in my life. This chapter was titled as such because God filters out the non-beneficial people and things in your life when you ask him for help. Not everybody can go where God wants to take us. My favorite book that relates to this subject is "The Alchemist." God had to get me in a quiet place where He could have my full attention. Finally, separating from their mother did not change my mentality when it pertained to the care and relationship with my boys. In fact, it motivated me to even do more. I told myself that now is the time to get back on my feet and grow into the image that I had envisioned for myself.

The Perfect Sip

Financial stability and happiness is what I've always strived for. In the mist of relationship drama, my second son gave me more life. Trayvon was a full-term baby, perfectly healthy and handsome like his older brother. Both of my boys looked like they could have been twins. The only difference between them were their eyes. Having children should give anybody life, but I don't understand how some parents choose to be absent from their kid's life from day one. Well, I take that back to some extent now that I'm older and see how parents treat each other in some cases. Point is some people are careless while having sex, make a child and continue being irresponsible in raising them. What's worse than being a child brought into this world having neither parent want them? That's trauma followed by drama. I couldn't do that to my kids because I have too much love and empathy for them. They give me life, energy and purpose. Whatever they

need within reason, they got it. I pay and stay current on child support. Parental love will change you from being selfish to selfless. Parental love will always make you work hard in order to provide and support them by any means. Parental love will make you come to terms with certain sacrifices that you may have to make for them. Parental love will make you want to give them the best life without spoiling or crippling them. I admit I was financially and emotionally crippled, licking my wounds as I returned home to my parent's house.

I was 27 at the time, I had no credit, no car, no savings, no relationship, and no job. I barely had any pride. What I did have was God, and with Him, I had hope, a restoration of faith and became more spiritually conscious than religious. I saw how He was doing what was necessary for my growth by repositioning me in life. I had to do a lot of soul-searching at the time which was beneficial to my

manhood. I had to pull myself together and remove the clutter from my life. Focusing on the reality of my situation, I basically had to internally make my own declaration of success and happiness while moving forth in taking advantage of the opportunity that was given to me to get back on my feet. My self-esteem and confidence increased as I saw God open doors that used to be shut on me. Along my personal journey, I learned that I must become my own crazy, loud cheerleader. You are in control of your thoughts and emotions. Yes, talk to yourself. Cheer for yourself. Speak life into your soul and spirit by making positive affirmations every day. If you don't, nobody will. Understand and accept that sometimes nobody will cheer for you if they can see or sense that you don't cheer and take care of yourself. Know that the power of the tongue is just that powerful. Similar to a prayer, when making affirmations, you are communicating

with the spirit of God within you seeking help for improvement. The difference between the two is rather than asking or thanking God in prayer, you are verbally making a command in the universe. The Bible states that even before God created light, it was His words that manifested creation. God said, "Let there be light" and there was light. I made a habit of making positive affirmations daily. My favorite affirmation is, "Filter my life Lord; give me your caffeine." Sounds weird? I am simply asking God for daily house cleaning services and replenishment of positive energy to do what He needs me to do. I like to say this after initially thanking God for allowing me to see another day. Try it or make your own personal affirmations. Either way, there is a supernatural power that takes place once that is proclaimed. The whole objective is recycling good energy in your life. What two better sources than God and coffee? "Filter my life

The Perfect Sip

Lord and give me your caffeine" is what I say as my daily prayer request. I thought about this when I made coffee the theme of this book. We all need positive mental and spiritual energy every day. Don't you agree? So, in my short prayer, I am simply asking for the removal of everything unnecessary so that I can take in the beneficial substances that I need to grow. I dare you to try this and see God at work. Say your affirmations as you make coffee. Say it while you are on the toilet or taking a shower. Say it on your way to work. Say it when you are happy or stressed. Say it at night before sleeping and when you wake up. Use the power of the tongue to speak life. All it takes is a verbal command with good intentions to control the physical realm by commands obeyed in the spiritual realm. Give all your worries to God and watch yourself feel better. Remember my prayer

slogan long after you finish this book. "Filter my life Lord and give me your caffeine."

Chapter 14:

Cravings

I feel that when God applied His filter to my life, He strained out a situation-ship that was mistaken for a relationship. God's filter provided clarity and exposed the truth. My main goal in my children's lives is not to be a dead-beat dad. Although their mother and I were not right for each other, I made a personal commitment to always be active in their lives no matter the hurdles. She does not make it easy always causing unnecessary drama. I had to acknowledge the fact that we only stayed together so long was for

stability and support while watching the kids grow. Basically, I was repeating the cycle that I saw while growing up. I began to feel like we were roommates rather than a couple living together. God had to remind me that the people are in my life for reasons and seasons. I have the free will to determine the people I allow into my life and to determine when I have outgrown them as well. I've learned how low self-esteem and depression can determine what you'll settle for. Sometimes, you'll just need to deal with people no matter how detrimental, just to not have nobody. We started out friends, but things just fell apart. I'm very much thankful for the two children that she has given me and pray that we can continue functioning as co-parents in the proper manner. There are a lot of people who are married and not happy, and I didn't want to be one of them. God prevented my spirit from being comfortable in my mess. If your life is not going the way you

envisioned, then you probably need to put a filter on it. That is my best advice. A filter will give you clarity, discernment, wisdom, and peace. God is the best filter in the market. Don't let misery make you a prisoner. Filter your life because you are worthy and deserve the best you can ever be.

The urge to be independent can prematurely thrust you into adulthood faster than you can imagine, so it is important to control your cravings. I encourage everyone to create a vision board along with an effective strategy toward accomplishing those goals. Create it, change it, and rearrange it if need be. That's exactly what I did. I was intentional and determined regardless of what my life looked like.

Here, I was back at my parents' house after successfully failing at my initial attempt at being grown. I fell flat on my face. Wrong relationship,

poor job employment, bad choices, mistakes and a lot of frustration. During this time, me and my younger brother, Alvin, returned back home also after years of independent dysfunctional living. Sam was not happy at the time but what can you say? Life happened and I couldn't help it. Regina gave us another chance to restart but informed us that it would be their last time helping us. My father gave us both seven months to get back on our feet and move out. This deadline was a bit difficult being that Columbia, TN was an even smaller town than Jackson, TN which meant that the salaries were somewhat lower. The first day I returned home, I got hired at the Olive Garden in Spring Hill, TN. I basically transferred from the location in Jackson, TN and I worked there for a good two months as a busser/server. My mother demanded that I save every penny from my tips and paychecks so that I could put a down payment on my own car. I did

just that and within a two-month period, I bought a 2007 Chevy Impala.

After purchasing my first car, I began seeking new employment because of the high car note. Three days later, God blessed me with my first job in hospitality as a front desk agent/night auditor for the Fairfield Inn and Suites owned by Marriott. This was a career field that I thrived in. I applied for several positions while living in Jackson, TN but never got hired. At that point, I knew that relocating was the answer to my employment struggle. Giving credit back to God's plan, I noticed that it takes having the willingness and bravery to be repositioned in life to reach fulfillment. Isn't it crazy how fear, uncertainty paralyzes you mentally and physically? Sometimes, God has to push you out of your clouds in order to show you what kind of storm you were in. Just let go and let God do His thing when it comes to His choice in the person,

places or things that are in your life. We often pray and ask God for help but if His help pertains to the removal of the main thing that you are not willing to let go of, then you are defeating the whole purpose. Help me to stop drinking, God! How can He be of help when you won't let anybody take the bottle from your hands? Help me to love again, God! How can He when you still won't let go of the person who is making you feel like crap? Help me to become wealthy, Lord! How can He help when you are lazy, don't apply yourself and are comfortable with being on welfare, section 8 and any other government assistance? Don't get me wrong, there is nothing wrong with government assistance, but there are many people who choose to settle for that lifestyle. Unfortunately, this lifestyle is mimicked and passed down to generation after generation rather than working hard. We can never have what God truly wants to give to us if we

The Perfect Sip

are constantly holding on to what is killing us. That was me all day. I was causing more injury to myself because I had a hard time letting go of the past.

Once I let go, I began to fall. That is what naturally happens. You fall, you hurt, you cry but faith will tap you on your shoulder when you are done and will ask you whether you are still up for the challenge. This is when determination gives you your custom-made wings. Determination to succeed will not only save you from hitting the ground and dying, but it will help you fly then soar. Your flight will look ugly and shaky at first, but as you pull yourself together in becoming in sync with the wind current of life. Your flight abilities will eventually begin looking smoother and more natural. That is the development of an eagle. They get hatched in a nest and when the parent feels that it is time for them to fly, they purposely make the nest very uncomfortable to the point where the young eagles

leave the nest in attempt to fly. I realized that all I had to do was move back home temporarily after graduating college and relocate to where I could thrive. The same progressive results would have manifested. Getting back to my new career in hospitality, I absolutely loved it being that I am a people person. Within a three-month period of moving back home, the blessings came back to back. I had a better car and a better job which made me tremendously happier. I felt like I was catching up to where I thought I should be as a 27-year-old adult. I was simply amazed at how quickly God was opening doors for me upon starting all over again. Although, I was not close toward being where I wanted to be, it was a significant change. My life was turning around.

People often say that things get worse before they get better, but I did not know the extent of the difficulty in that matter. As my seven-month

deadline to evacuate the house approached, I was still not financially stable enough to move out on my own. Nine and ten dollars per hour jobs were not cutting it for me especially since child support was coming out of my check, which prompted me to get another job. As I worked two jobs, my life definitely got more difficult. I ended up seeking a night auditor job at the Baymont which resulted in me working 16-hour shifts, five days out of the week. It was hard on my body, and it did tell on me. My work cycle consisted of working 16 hours and sleeping for six. I hardly had time for anything else because I was tired all the time, always playing catch up on sleep.

Rather than working harder, I knew I had to work smarter. Instead of working two low salaried jobs that was killing me, I chose to branch out farther toward the city for better pay so that I could work one job. I was successful with getting hired at

a hotel property in Franklin, TN. The job couldn't have come at a better time being that my dad stuck with his decision in the time he allowed me to stay there. My brother had moved out to stay with his girlfriend a few months prior to me getting kicked out. For the first time in my life, I was homeless on my own, and that was a bit scary. I kept my head up and what kept me calm was the fact that I had my own transportation to work and I was making more money. I knew that I could survive as long as I had those two tools. Moving out, I transferred my belongings into a climate-controlled storage unit. I paid to have 24-hour access so that I would come and go as I pleased. The benefits of a climate-controlled storage unit are that it served as a shelter when needed. If I didn't have a couch to sleep on at a friend's house, I would sleep in my 10 x 15 ft unit on an air mattress. If I did not sleep there, I slept in the back seat of my Impala that had tinted

The Perfect Sip

windows. During that time, I made sure to keep my $20 a month Planet Fitness membership. This gave me access to bathrooms and showers so I could maintain good hygiene and keep myself groomed. I could take long showers and not have to worry about a high water bill. I could exercise whenever I wanted to, watch T.V without having to worry about a cable bill and I could get unlimited massage therapy with the massage chairs and the hydro massage water beds. I had a 24-hour access to all of that for just 20 dollars a month. Talk about survival, right. Some nights at my new job, my managers would allow me to spend a few nights in a room depending on the occupancy of the hotel during the week.

For six months, I was homeless and didn't have my own place or where I could call my own. I wasn't a dirty begging bum like we normally see, rather I just needed more time to save to get on my

feet once again. Nobody could tell that I was homeless by my appearance and attitude. People only knew my business if I told them. All I had was God, my car, job, storage unit, and Planet Fitness membership. This was how I survived throughout my challenging times. I think of it as my five-month wilderness experience. God had my undivided attention, and in return, He gave me peace in the reassurance that this was all happening for a reason and everything was going to be ok. While saving, making progress, and patiently waiting on God to map out a detour, my spirit remained at ease. My spirit was very humble. I was not angry nor suicidal for some reason. Some things are just supernaturally unexplainable which why I continuously acknowledge God because he serves as the "X-Factor" in the equation of life. God also made sure that I was conscious of who was there for me and who wasn't. I hit rock bottom, and there was no

The Perfect Sip

family in sight. I later found out that while I was homeless, my mother moved my sons and their mother into their house. Nobody told me about it, I just happened to find out-out of the blue one day. I felt replaced and substituted but was glad that my boys had reliable shelter. Out of the six-month period of being on my own, my mom only offered help to me once by giving me 20 dollars that I asked her for food. It appeared as if she was finished with me and had moved on to my sons and having the daughter (mother of my kids), she never was able to have. It also appeared that my adoptive mother and the mother of my kids took delight in my struggle. Sometimes, people only feel good when they can make you feel bad. Phone calls were ignored, text messages were rarely responded to, nobody called to check on me, and nobody even offered a bed or a roof over my head even for one night. I paid attention to how I was treated while being at my

lowest. This realization gave me the backbone and mental ability to shun everybody who was not there for me in my trial times. I took it for what it was as I continued to better my situation. Unaware of God's plan, I trusted Him in the midst of my struggle. He was basically removing the people who meant no good to me in my life. I didn't know it then, but I was headed to the next level. I was isolated to gain clarity. Consciously, I believe that God wanted me all to Himself so that nobody could take credit toward my transformation but Him. He saw the best in me. I was not homeless in His eyes, rather I was simply placed on standby as He prepared me for the blessings in store for me.

Chapter 15:

Sweet Life

We all crave the "Good Life", right? The good life is our vision of the perfect lifestyle that we so desire. What would you do if you hit the lottery? I believe everybody wants to have the time, energy and finances to live however they want. I know I did. In addition to time and financial freedom, I desired a life full of good experiences. With persistent effort, I was able to improve my situation. I kept saving money while still taking care of myself. God was with me in every step which is why I can testify to His greatness. The

Shay EL

more progress I made, the happier I became. He saw my effort and answered my prayers like many times before. If God was for me then who would be against me? Having God's favor was like being untouchable. My faith in Him gave me the peace and inner confidence that I needed to stay mentally strong. Understand that God's timing is perfect, and we must continue striving toward our goals while patiently waiting for the right doors to be open. I kept praying specifically in detail for the things I wanted in my life. I literally did this faithfully and my whole life changed for the better. Prayer still works and it was evident during the roughest part of my transition in life as God sent me help.

God sent me the sweetest woman by the name Kori. We met at work. Now, let me tell you up front our stories on how we met and who hollered at who. We laugh and joke about it all the time, but I'm about to tell you my side. Kori let her interest

The Perfect Sip

to be known through a co-worker who interrogated me out the blue one day. She point-blank asked me if I was married, gay, had a girlfriend or a crazy baby mama who thinks she is my girlfriend. Caught off guard, I paused and asked who was it that was interested in me and wanted to know such personal information. When she told me who it was, and I just smiled, because we had already been cheesing at each other every morning, both too nervous to actually approach the other. She was beautiful, had a great vibe, seemed genuine and had a nice shape. She was thicker than Georgia cotton to be exact. She worked for the hospital that rented out the second floor of the hotel for sleep studies. The day we officially introduced ourselves to each other came one morning a few weeks later, as we crossed paths during our shift change. We spoke briefly in the hallway and exchanged numbers and well as each other's social media info. We talked for a while

before going out on any dates. We both agreed on our desire to just be happy and be loved sincerely. It's scary when you meet the person of your dreams. You almost don't get your hopes up in fear of disappointment. It's that too good to be true feeling. When God adds to your life, He adds without sorrow and that's how you know it's from Him.

Our first six months was definitely a test. God tested our patience, loyalty, commitment, attitude, anger management and respect for one another. These are the important tool-like principles needed to build relationships that last. My relationship with Kori has always felt like a good fairy tale. Our goofy, corny personalities synced perfectly like the right puzzle pieces. God gave us each other for a reason. We were each other's healer. Kori was proposed to by four different men years after her divorce from her first marriage and yet she chose to

The Perfect Sip

marry me. How was I the lucky guy that she said yes to? Only God knows but she did. It made me feel special. We accepted each other for who we were and what we have been through. We vowed to make each other better. So many people have told us that our love was inspiring, but many prayed against us as well. Our supporters said we were cute together. Haters would say the awful things like, "Oh, he found himself a sugar momma," or "she's old, fat and just wants a young tenderoni." The truth is that we have each other's back and love each other. Haters need to focus on their own problems and figure out the cause of their own misery. Can't stand how people try to contaminate and pollute another person's relationship. Whether we last or not, we will be friends for life. We were simply two broken people with traumatizing past of abuse who attempted to love and heal one another.

Once again people come into your life for reasons and seasons. Discern the two.

We are progressive and always on the move. It's kind of neat how we used different means of transportation for each special moment of our union. We took a train ride to our proposal at the DelMonaco Winery, a plane ride to Las Vegas for our wedding and a Cruise Ship to Jamaica for our honeymoon. For our proposal, we had a wine tasting train ride to the vineyard, so we were giddy to say the least, especially Kori. She is a lightweight when it comes to drinking. The staff members orchestrated my vision to perfection. Below us stood hundreds of spectators who attended the tour that day. They were all secretly informed of the proposal as well. Excitement created a buzz in the atmosphere. I made my grand proposal to her on a balcony with a live band playing, and it went perfectly as planned. The crowd that stood below

The Perfect Sip

us was cheering, crying, and recording the moment with their phones. Strangers bought wine bottles for us while we were there, and we got showered with love as they congratulated us on the train ride back to Nashville. It was an amazing and a memorable moment that I will cherish forever. I had wanted the day that I will propose to my wife to be special, and I thank God for making that possible. The execution was perfect.

Seven months later, we flew to Las Vegas to get married. We stayed at the beautiful Venetian where we enjoyed the weekend loving on each other. No bad vibes, no bad energy, just the two of us making our commitment to each other before God. Three weeks later, we boarded the Carnival Vista for our seven-day honeymoon cruise. It was my first cruise, and I loved it. The ship was huge, fun and very relaxing. I loved the food, spa packages, entertainment and the comfort that I experienced. I

was turned on to the cruise life. For seven days, we got to experience the blessing of just being alone together and free. For the first time in my life, I felt genuine freedom. I felt on top of the world and like I had finally made it. Kori and I made it our goal to cruise around yearly. For our one-year anniversary, we went to Honduras, Costa Maya, Cozumel Mexico, and Belize to tour the Mayan ruins. It was so beautiful. Experiencing the world outside the country has given me a greater appreciation for other cultures and for the things that we have access to in the United States. I encourage everyone to get out and experience the world. Not only is traveling fun but the world is beautiful despite how television depicts certain places. Get out and see the world. Go solo, with friends, or your significant other. Create memories to cherish and use pictures as souvenirs. Life is short so enjoy it.

Chapter 16:

GoodAddiction

Believe it or not, God wants us to live a happy, meaningful life. I know life is difficult but everything we go through is to make us stronger and wiser. We were not born to live in misery. Now we may struggle from time to time, but we are supposed to eventually get the understanding of what is required to make our lives better.

With that being said, I created my brand called, "GoodAddiction", to consciously promote the awareness and importance of mental health. You must love yourself. You can't be a service to the world if you are not well from within. Nobody likes a "Scrooge".

Now that things have come full circle, I crave happiness and choose to be hooked on that emotion. Take a second to think about what truly makes you happy. Having difficulty? Well, "GoodAddiction", represents the creativity of healthy lifestyles through the balance of doing what makes you happy. Following your soul is the best way to find your "Good" addiction.

It's happiness period, no compromises. Isn't that a good affirmation to repeat to yourself? The sooner we understand the control we have over our emotions he happier we will be. We have a choice.

The Perfect Sip

This starts by choosing the right people to be in your circle and sometimes changing your environment

My success has come from my relationship with God in addition to the desire of wanting to be fulfilled. Success is all about adapting to change and taking action. Have you ever rudely yelled at someone who was in your way out of inpatients or frustration? Why? They were in the way, slowing down your pace, preventing you from moving further right? Well, now is the time to do that to yourself with the same forceful energy. The people who I use to be around were underachievers, negative, broke, miserable, controlling, compulsive liars and master manipulators. Their lifestyles and attitudes did not influence nor inspire me.

If you have not heard by now, you become a product of your environment. Although I was

amongst them, I did not want to settle for the lifestyle that they were comfortable in. I knew that I had to raise my standards out of respect for myself to see a change in every circumstance. I was tired of struggling, being broke, and being around people who had poverty mindsets. I just had a different vision for my life. I wanted more. My vision was all about greatness rather than being average. I would literally tell myself, "Move Shay, stop complaining and take more action." "More action, less talking". "More action, less thinking". "More action, less worrying". "More action, less procrastinating".

To be great, you must do more period. This requires getting out of your comfort zone. Meditating daily has given me the motivation needed to make necessary changes in my life on a consistent basis. This helps with focus and clarity. I began isolating myself. Despite silence from

The Perfect Sip

distractions, I had to be my own cheerleader and hype man to take back control of my happiness.

A bad trait I had was feeling the need to always please people. Even when they cared less about me, I was a prisoner to other people's thoughts and opinions about me. This came from years in foster care having to please care givers to make them like and want to keep me. Through prayer, God told me to care more about the plans that He had for me. My focus needed to be on God therefore I made the switch. Who is better to get clarity from? God was trying to get me on my path to fulfillment, but I was living for the approval from family, friends, and peers. Why?

Like many, we want that validation and encouragement from them. What I found out was that people in my life were only happy if they could control me. If I wasn't beneficial to them, they

could care less about me. Focusing on God and His plan will provide you with the spiritual armor that will protect you from the backstabbing that is sure to come once you get ahead. When people can't figure out how you made it and got ahead, they'll start lying about your existence and progress. Prepare for it. Don't be discouraged as you may wonder why certain people are not genuinely supportive of you. Live for the principles that matter to you the most. That's what I did, and my whole life changed for the better.

Today, I walk with my head high with a smile on my face. I am more confident, my faith is abundant, and I love my relationship with God. My trials and triumphs continue to shape and mold me into my greatest version. More importantly I understand the importance of obeying God's plan. Whatever God has for you is for you. Nobody can stop that but you.

The Perfect Sip

I personally like making highlight journals of all the ups and downs that occur throughout the year. I have been doing this since 2013, and I'm reaping the results now. Documenting blessings throughout the years will strengthen your faith. Sometimes, you have to look back and see how far you've come to be grateful for where you are at the moment. God's side is the good side, and when you walk in His mercy, grace, favor, and protection, you become unstoppable. That is how I feel daily. Unstoppable!! Wearing my own brand apparel brings me so much joy because I created something that is bigger than me that serves a purpose.

I encourage you to put forth positive energy into whatever you choose to create. The universe will respond accordingly when you do so. Your energy and vibe are part of the universal language. People can feel it without speaking your language. Your vibe is powerful, and God's universe responds to it.

I speak on this because your energy is the fuel that you will consistently need in manifesting your personal visions. Keep it in check at all times. Your life is the way that it is because of your choices, energy, and vibe. I love being the representation of good vibes, good energy, prosperity, and happiness. That is my good addiction, and that is why my brand means so much to me. In addition to the happiness that it brought, God has provided the wealth earnings also.

Wealth is created by aligning yourself with the purpose and plan God has for your life. That's is the best way I explain it. God is the key to wealth. Forget being rich. All I know is that it takes obedience, effort, discipline and faith. Don't follow what other people are doing because that may not be for you. I love how Jesus went into the desert alone to fast, receive instructions and to communicate with God. Moses did the same thing

when he fled Egypt. Both had to isolate themselves in order to get instructions from God. Therefore, know that it is ok to be alone sometimes.

Easier said than done right? It's a struggle for me as well. The first time my wife and I went to marriage counseling the therapist advised us to individually see trauma therapist after her evaluation. We both need inner healing. We both experienced traumatic situations in our youth that still affect us as adults today. It is a working progress but I'm learning how to overcome abandonment trauma. I never knew my biological parents but through the grace of God they are still alive and well. I plan on getting to know them personally to fill and heal that void within. The therapist instructed us to take the time to work on ourselves so that we can become our best versions for each other.

Distractions must go, people and family members must go, social media must go, the news must go, and even television shows must go sometimes. Why? God needs that intimate time with you so that He can walk with you and work on you. He wants to reveal the vision He has for you. That's why I love silence. You can hear and feel God speaking to your conscious when things are quiet. Everything that surrounds us has a certain energy to it. I love my peace so much that I often drive in silence. God has so much in store for us, but we often miss it because our minds are distracted and cluttered by worldly things. Your mind becomes too loud. Remember that your purpose is your business and it should be guarded seriously. It is up to you to take charge and run it. Lastly, your life is a result of your ritual addictions, so make them good and be prepared to take the perfect sip.

P.s…After 30 years of life, I am very excited about meeting with my biological mother, father and siblings in person for the first time. I need to know where and who I came from. Life is too short for grudges, so I have a trip planned to meet them, and I can't wait to tell you about it. Love you all and stay tuned for the second sip to see what happened a year later. Also please do me a favor and recommend this book to those who may be inspired by it as well. My mission is to place this book in every foster care center, orphanage, halfway house, and in the homes of adoptive families for inspiration. Thank you! Be blessed.

Benediction

There are five things that I want you to take away from my book that I will share with you now.

1. Every single person that we encounter in life serves a purpose in helping us become our optimal selves, even the demons. I encountered abusers, murderers & pedophiles along the way that taught me discernment. I've had good teachers, a foster sister and wife that showed me love. They (and all others in between) were all necessary in getting me to where I needed to be. Romans 8:28
2. In life, we never really lose. It's either we win, or we learn. I needed my bottom of the barrel experience. Homelessness & suffering was the

activation to my greatest inner strength. Being knocked down so hard allowed me the opportunity to become intimate with God. God was then able to show me that He was truly all that he needed to succeed. Psalm 16:5-11.

3. Your beginning does not dictate your end. This is self-explanatory, it just means that no matter where you start in life, with God and a little perseverance you can make it. Just keep moving forward. Job 8:7

4. Writing is therapy. Sometimes, there are things that we deal with in life that are too hard to talk about. Writing them down, and then going back to review how far you have come is a form of therapy. Writing is also a beautiful way to chart your goals and milestones of achievements. Record them as highlights every year for recollection. So, write, write, write! Let your desires be known to the Lord. Habakkuk 2:2

5. Good addictions. It is important to be addicted to things that are positive and beneficial to your life. Love yourself and put

your happiness first. No compromises. Daily affirmations can manifest into a lifetime of peace and happiness. Philippians 4:8.

I hope that this book blesses you along your journey.

www.ingramcontent.com/pod-product-compliance
Lightning Source LLC
Chambersburg PA
CBHW022103160426
43198CB00008B/335